Revolution
by
Cliché

Books by David Cort

DAVID CORT

❧⟨❀⟩❧

Revolution
by
Cliché

❧⟨❀⟩❧

FUNK & WAGNALLS · NEW YORK

Note

The divergent coordinates for the ensuing exploration were provided by Carey McWilliams, Victor Navasky, and Gustave Flaubert. If there is credit, they share it; if there is blame, they are absolved. Any burden of misfeasance is reserved solely to the author.

Contents

Directive

The one boast that can be made for this inquiry is that it is not (repeat, not) definitive.

One will find no attempt to close forever the subject of clichés, or any of the subsidiary areas opened. On the contrary, the intent, probably hopeless, is to open the matter so wide that it can never be quite entirely closed again.

Subjects are closed, as in most textbooks, by listing the parts of the whole, to be memorized and parroted back in the final examination, enforcing the assumption that the parts of the whole, by simple arithmetic, must add up to the whole. But the professor who writes the textbook does not know the whole and is unable to describe it. If he tries to describe it, he ruins his academic career. The whole is never a list of parts. But the professor can dismiss this opinion with one short cliché word: gestalt.

Subjects are opened by attempting, however ineptly, to describe the whole, which in most serious affairs is usually indescribable. Such attempts, as here, are subject to attack in detail, itemized from the professor's list of the parts, spread out on the garage floor. Most subjects are more complex than an automobile's works. But only in the attempt to describe the whole can anybody be taught the line between the known and the unknown or the perhaps unknowable.

The fallacy verging on pure evil in modern pedagogy is that the teacher really knows what he is talking about. His demand that the precisely defined parts of a subject be memorized has the marvelous effect of stopping thought. But if the students are invited to try to grasp the whole, before they are given the parts, they must be drawn into uncertain, desperate, and even original thought, which may take them a little closer to the understanding of the whole (and failure in the professor's final examination on details). This latter mind will be educated; the former will not.

The current educational apparatus produces few real educations, for few are demanded by the young careerists, not to speak of the riotous children who will be considered later. The cliché has become that a youth is more or less educated today if he has even heard of Charlemagne or Achilles. If he knows about Menelaus or Aetius or Montrose, he is getting his master's in history and plans to teach. Whom?

The above does not justify the revolting youth, who obviously do not know what it is they don't know. What follows will make happy neither the journalistic-educational-governmental-legal Establishment, nor the youths who are making it unhappy. The former has time to reform; the latter very little time, if any.

Revolt in some form is at present chic, that is, a cliché, that is, a joke, lacking precise meaning. But revolution is serious business, and so it has always been regarded by Americans. America has had a number of non-joke revolutions, and the Constitution still stands, and will probably continue to stand. Revolution is not a joke, or lark. Some of the joke revolutions are identified in the following pages, for the Establishment has forgotten how to laugh.

The American Revolution was based on truths so visceral that they have not become clichés in two hundred years, which is a long time. This is not to say that revolution by cliché, that is, by half-truths, cannot succeed, for it has brilliantly done so, briefly. The clichés of the French, Russian, Italian, and German revolutions have long since dried into empty and horrid husks, but men marched to them with swelling faith and pride, on, on, to degradation and death. For these glorious revolutions, the cliché saying "Welcome!" was the doormat before the pit, with slaves.

Some sophistication about the cliché, the half-truth, the imprecise political promise, is required of every citizen of a democracy. How anybody can or ever could compare the American Revolution, Declaration, and Constitution with any Russian revolution scripted by Marx, Lenin, Stalin, and prefer the latter and betray the former, is a mystery whose only solution is that these people must be stupid, ignorant, or debased. Since some high-minded, educated people have still preferred the Communist Revolution, they are probably not all three, only one or two, but the meaning of "debased" must be given wide latitude, encompassing everything from vicious to crazy, including ambitious, Caesaristic, conspiratorial, fratricidal, satanic, and paranoiac. All these are closed and obsessed compulsions, not entirely understood, not precisely defined, and so clichés.

In fact, in Communist, Fascist or Nazi societies, the individual human being is a cliché, a stereotype, a nothing. Given the nature of man and of power, the elimination of nothing is easy and natural in such a society; thus, mass killing becomes the totalitarian cliché.

The killing may be a cliché; death is never a cliché, for as the individual's heart stops, the whole unexplored network of the individual's relationships dies in its tracks. The stopping of one heart kills unassessable meanings in an unguessable number of lives. The reverberation of the cliché killing rolls on unpredictably and awfully, a fact by no means overlooked by Stalin and Hitler.

These survivors of the cliché, Russians, Italians, Germans, Chinese, *et al.*, must have lost all feeling in the hearts which mechanically go on pumping—horrors!— blood. To some degree, they become the walking dead. From the great revolutionary clichés, we have inherited on all the streets of the world the walking dead.

The American Revolution, on the other hand, brought people to life. Its ideas have brought to life the walking dead from other lands, turned frogs into princes, and revealed for all further time the latent aristocracies sleeping in former serfs. These ideas cannot be clichés.

But princes do not like to be remembered as ex-frogs, or the living as ex-walking dead, or aristocrats as ex-serfs. Because the magic was so easy, it was no magic. And so America has been subjected to a massive fit of ingratitude. The beneficiaries insist that America is a cliché, and that the jobs in this most intricate complex of powers ever created are unworthy of their newly discovered talents. America is suddenly unworthy of these parvenus. Some of these will be specified in these pages.

The current disillusion with the American system will end, paradoxically, when the current affluence ends. Certainly nobody can believe that the gala will go on forever, or much longer. Then the demand for jobs that "fulfill" the individual will cease abruptly. The brain lobe now luxuriating in disillusion will return to its basic function of realistic anxiety.

The current revolts of youth all over the world may be a sensitive reaction to the fact that they are *fin de siècle*, and that this is their last chance. For youth is especially sensitive to social excesses and dislocations and hypocrisies. Youth wants to believe. Now, suspecting that their future is not going to be ideal, rather idiotically they add to the hypocrisies, excesses, and dislocations. Well, after all, it is their future, not mine. I can laugh; they cannot. But in fact they are laughing and I am not.

The current American youth would be shocked to hear that a thousand years from now, America, explicitly the United States, will be remembered as a strange, reckless, perhaps doomed experiment in total faith in mankind. What will have doomed it cannot be said today; perhaps the lawyers, perhaps the politicians, perhaps the accountants, perhaps the scientists, or, perhaps, the youth.

Historians in the year A.D. 2900 will decide what doomed the great American experiment. But the criminals need not cringe; by then they will all be dead. The victims of their crime will be their posterity, whom they had not thought of. But posterity will think of them snug in their graves, and if they have the strength, they will curse them.

But aha! Perhaps the experiment is not doomed; perhaps it will simply submerge and outwit and transcend all the jokers, villains, ingrates now in attendance. The American democracy will again explode out of the

closed clichés, which will be swallowed up in the tran-
scendent whole again, and again. I think America is a
natural phenomenon, indescribable as a whole, greater
than the sum of its parts, a continuing event that will
always defy any cliché. It is not closed, and cannot be
closed.

But aha! Look again. America is filled with very
clever men. The devices for reducing Americans to
happy submission (some explored in these pages) are
the common coin of these clever men. Nothing said here
will surprise them at all. Free Americans might do
well to consider the *coup d'état* without political or
military support, as recently in Greece and elsewhere.
Under specific conditions it would also be possible, not
easy, not imminent, in the United States. For there is
now a ghastly thing called Intelligence. It was formerly only G-2; now it is the CIA and all sorts of allied
and satellite organizations which collect information,
not intelligence, and, seduced by the word, suppose that
they are intelligent. They thus cannot help project our
destiny or refrain from wanting to impose it on us. I
have known these people; in a way, I am one of them.
They exist.

What would happen in case of such a coup? Immediately, the whole rehearsed and perfected apparatus of
protest, by the youth and the Negroes, one would hope,
would explode. The very people whom I have dis-
counted in these pages would become, perhaps, our
first line of defense. This protest, unfortunately, would
be only a preliminary skirmish, easily swept aside, but
perhaps decisively intimidating to Intelligence. It might
be that easy, but it might not. In the latter case, the
whole American people, the squares, the honkies, the

very people the youth and Negroes deplore, would have to do the job. What do you think? Would you do it?

The subject, as one can see, is wide open, not closed.

Smart people will infer from the following pages that I am a fool. But I know that the way to lose all power is to tell the whole truth one knows. One throws oneself on the mercy of a merciless court or, in poker, turns all one's cards face up, against desperate players with closed hands. I know this. Yet my hope is that these inquiries will conclude in my perfect bankruptcy.

Revolution
by
Cliché

❧ 1 ❧

The Received Idea

Waiting patiently to be rediscovered by a new generation always lies the terrible recognition that language is a fairly poor medium of communication. An instant later comes the frightening intuition that there are no meanings, and then the suspicion that everybody has been lying. A simple lexicological insight often leads to astonishing uproars, as if everybody had somehow been betrayed. The current "alienation" and "loss of identity" are part of this process.

A return to first principles may restore some calm. Language is indeed a poor medium. It is artificial; it is not instinctive; it has to be learned. The words do not radiate their meanings. Words can be only labels for what is already known to both parties in the communication. Colors, sounds, tastes, motions can only be labeled. The word yellow is not itself yellow; the word spiral is not spiral; the European words for the flavors

1

vanilla and chocolate would have been gibberish before the sixteenth century, because Europeans had not
yet found vanilla and chocolate in the New World.
Light is meaningless to those born blind; sound to those
born deaf. In the familiar nonscientific language, many
words are nonsense to people who do not know history
and geography, or to those who don't know the classical
myths or the Bible. A word is a convention and means
what people agree it means.

Words are not mechanically built from the twenty-
six letters of our alphabet. Anagram players are especially aware that there are millions of possible combinations that are not included in a large English dictionary
of some six hundred thousand words. This same alphabet accommodates dozens of other languages, with few
duplications, and with plenty of leeway left for more
languages, as needed.

Words grow out of ideas, evolved, combined, and corrupted, in stems, prefixes, and suffixes. A stem such as
"tain," corrupted from the Latin *tenere,* to hold, produces attain, contain, detain, entertain, maintain, ob-
tain, retain, sustain. The number of basic ideas forming
English words is a small fraction of dictionary words.

The most savage attack on language ever composed
is certainly James Joyce's *Finnegans Wake.* Seeming
senseless, its use of simultaneous clichés paradoxically
ends in a marvelous exactness of implication for the
well-educated reader. "Whets the wits . . . dogs'
death, bitches' birth . . . entails the ensuance . . .
That song sang seaswans . . . overhoved, shrillglee-
screaming . . . wasterpaperbaskel . . ." and so on,
play chords across the whole keyboard of Western culture and mock its pretense at communication. The

young like the general message, but they can no more understand this than they can Marcel Proust, until they know a little more.

James Joyce was certainly not the first to discover the absurdity of language. Poets have been exquisitely sensitive to the inadequacy of the tools they are given, and therefore combine words that make literal nonsense but may, they hope, suggest something close to a recognizable fantasy they had had in mind, such as "Opening on the foam of perilous seas in faery lands forlorn." This succession of phrases seems to describe a place subconsciously familiar to some, but not found in standard geographies.

If everybody memorized Keats's line and kept quoting it to prove his spirituality, it would become a cliché. Only imagine a man with a thick regional or ethnic accent quoting it, and the marvelous phrase is dead.

In Keats's expression it will be noticed that every adjective and noun has several dictionary meanings. The statement is not exact or authoritatively definable. The words, simultaneously echoing all their possible meanings, are not single notes, but chords.

Such diapasons are of small use to ordinary people engaged in ordinary communication. When they say "automobile," they do not mean to suggest everything that is "self-moving," a condition that describes nearly all living animals. In their language, everybody knows what an automobile is, despite the infelicity of the word label.

Ordinary people, untroubled by lexicology, generally communicate in word combinations that they have repeatedly heard, that have lost precise meaning and are therefore clichés.

The first reason for using a cliché is to avoid argument. Formerly one said, "I'm regular, like the next guy." Later it was, "Yeah, man, I dig you." Both convey exactly the same message, in different times and groups, but to examine the literal meanings of the words employed would be entirely irrelevant. Both avoid any carefully considered opinion, in exact honesty, on what had been said before, and thus evade offense and argument. A cliché generalization taken from the current journalism of the area is the safest statement to make at a strange bar-and-grill.

For the press lives on the cliché and rejoices in it; it is generally uncomfortable with reality. In today's New York City newspaper the big black headline roars N.J. BRUNETTE FOUND SLAIN. As a cliché, this news is important. Below, in much smaller type, the paper nods toward what is really going on: *8,000 Dead in Iran Quake.* Eight thousand versus one "N.J. brunette," who was not caught in the shuddering of the great Asiatic rift, but only in some local evil. And the cliché triumphs. At the local bar, you had better say, "How about that dame over in Jersey?" not "Terrible about that earthquake in Iran."

Another reason for the cliché is as a passport into the clique. "One swell foop," the Spoonerism from Macduff's grievous cry, will signal to the mocking literate that one is one of them. "Independent as a hog on ice" will do the same for northern rustics and the rich who imitate the rustics. "So, what else is new?" is generally useful.

Another cliché, called jargon, is the tool of various bureaucracies, notably in the universities, and has a much more sinister intent, as will be explored in some detail later. This affects to make the process of thinking a professional ritual reserved to professional thinkers, and quite beyond the powers of anyone not versed in the jargon. These self-defined experts thus make thought their monopoly. Even without a law to legalize the monopoly, they run on as if they had an exclusive base of power. At the most ordinary level, there may be people who use the words cognate and substantive innocently, but I doubt it. ("Cognate" literally means related on the mother's side; the adjective "substantive" has nine diverse meanings.) Despite the monopoly, everybody can be assumed to go on thinking for himself, without jargon. But this is not an entirely sound assumption. The experts' jargon filters into the press, and finally reaches the ordinary citizen as acceptable cliché.

Words are far too omnivalent in meaning for communication, but as a replacement, clichés have no certifiable meaning. They are signals, not meanings. They suppress the word's history in depth, and simply wigwag a contemporary cue. They resemble the songs and calls of birds, which are also probably clichés, as are certainly the sounds issued by fish, shrimp, frogs, bats, bees, mosquitoes, and other insects. There is a current scientific intuition that only the dolphin knows what he is talking about.

Quail are not enraged to revolt against the monotonous "bob-white" of their elders. But mankind is more easily bored, and may revolt against the dominant clichés. These revolts, one of which is going on today, have no great stamina.

The more serious revolutions are founded on clichés. Just as individuals use clichés to play on one another's simplicity, politicians do the same thing on a mass scale. And in the world by which we are ruled, or manipulated, clichés are written large across human history. A few of these which have fairly recently piped men down to death and despair are ready to hand. For the subject of clichés is far from frivolous.

First, Lenin perfected what can be simplified as the stupendous Marxist lie that there is only one significant person in this world, the proletarian. If this is true (it is not), no more than one political party is necessary or, indeed, thinkable, for the proletariat is the only group that deserves representation. To this beauty, Lenin added, "Let's stop fighting for the Czar" (who had already been deposed). The Germans were promptly replaced by other shooting enemies, and the Russians went on fighting for Lenin. A reliable cliché, "Land for everybody," completed the package. Of course the Russians never got the land. If they had, it would have ceased to be a cliché. The people also wanted a representative government, which was forcibly ejected by Trotsky's Red Guards, for Lenin had added another idea, "They are incapable of representative government." Bolshevik Russia was then saved by the United States, not for the last time, as America crushed Imperial Germany.

Around 1920 Mussolini, an attentive observer of Lenin, read some Italian clichés: "Consumers don't like labor strikes," "Organized violence is persuasive to most people," and "Italians are tired of liberty. They need Order, Authority, Discipline." By then Lenin's idea that the people are incapable of representative government had become an accepted cliché.

Later Hitler read the clichés "Germany deserves to

be great," "Organized violence is convincing" and "The Jews are too smart." With a dilettante's acumen, he had also sensed that Europe didn't want to fight for anything. With these insights, Hitler lasted twelve years.

Much of this grisly politics rode on the cliché that party hacks want to keep their jobs. When Lenin died, Trotsky was helpless because Stalin owned the party hacks. In America, the President normally controls the party hacks and can renominate himself, even if he is Herbert Hoover. In every case the public welfare, or patriotism, is not enough.

It is obvious that the cliché may have an element of truth, but its important function is to exclude unamenable reality. In 1917 a great many Russians sincerely wanted to stop fighting Germans, but twenty-four years later here came the Germans again. The Russians really wanted land, but they didn't get it from the Bolsheviks; instead, they got death. The Fascisti were fairly good at violence, but not good enough for the world they were in. Germany deserved to be great but not that great. Smart German Jews might have helped Germany. The democracies were somewhat decadent, in a sense, but not that decadent. The clichés didn't quite work. The fraction of truth wasn't enough.

But there is an irresistible tendency to translate the real problems of a society into clichés that stereotype selected aspects of the reality into familiar forms that will stir sections of the people into emotion and action. The present aspirations of the Negroes, expressed by their various champions, are an adequate example. The tragedy is that once the clichés have been fossilized, government, that is, politicians, can deal with the problem only as cliché, not as complex reality. A direct, fresh, original reaction to the observed reality would ruin the politician. The politician wants only to offer his received idea, not to debate the realities. For he wants to be liked by the 51 per cent, as he figures, who already believe in his cliché, which he has essentially taken from his understanding of his constituency or following. Thus one can fairly conclude that it is we, the people, the sovereign power, who are to blame for our misfortunes, in signaling the corrupt cliché to the idiotic mouthpiece in the legislature. The Communist peoples, on the other hand, need feel no such guilt.

Clichés come in several forms. Idea clichés, which will occupy the forepart of this study, are by far the most dangerous. There will be time later to come to the relatively harmless metaphor-simile clichés, the life-style clichés, and the far-from-innocent vocabulary, or jargon-clichés.

Obviously the word cliché is used here in other than its vulgar sense. For the word itself has become a cliché. When someone says, "That old cliché, 'Honesty is the best policy,' " he is not using a cliché, he is giving the signal that he knows it is a hackneyed expression. The test of a cliché is that it is a signal conveying more or less (and sometimes both) than the literal meaning of the words. The expression just quoted is no more a cliché than "Honor thy father and thy mother that thy days may be long in the land which the Lord thy God giveth thee," though in some circumstances both might be used as signals, rather than as serious and traditional philosophies, since both are now nearly obsolete, except among a certain elite. The word cliché is now used in self-conscious snobbery or self-defense, a sophistication rarely used by the sophisticated. It is most frequently heard on TV conversation programs today.

The old definition of cliché is exhaustively explored by Eric Partridge's *A Dictionary of Clichés,* first published in 1940, now a long time ago. Among his examples of clichés are: far and wide, for good and all, null and void, ways and means, through and through, might and main, rack and ruin, high and dry, by and large, last but not least, moot point, status quo. Most of these are listed in a large dictionary, that is, they are basic building blocks of the language. Typically their meaning is more, not less, explicit than a single-word equivalent, as "by and large" for "generally" or "high and dry" for "stranded."

Mr. Partridge categorizes these as "hackneyed phrases," "hackney" meaning an ordinary horse or carriage for hire, hence worn down by common use. True, Partridge's expressions do not inspire fresh thought. But they are not signals of any kind, they cover situations adequately, and they constitute a definite if dull style. They are not, in the present view, clichés. They are simply language, like "Hello," "Goodbye," and "Sincerely yours." In some groups a cliché signal today would be "Your ob'd'nt servant."

As a signal gaining admission to a group, the cliché as signal is part of the social process. To label these signals clichés is an act of unwarranted snobbery toward the group. This is revealed by Partridge when he describes cliché-collecting as a "blood sport" (itself a signal cliché for a certain group). And this expression too is in the dictionary. The subject of clichés may call for pity and fury, but not merely snobbish malice.

The connoisseur of the new cliché should look to the

universities, where a tortured intellectual narcissism is rampant among the junior faculty. Thus an MIT professor in riot-time was asked, "Do you want to make the world a better place?" He responded entirely in the new, subtle clichés: "You have asked me an awful and kind of real question. [Get it? He has signaled his deep sincerity and suffering, on stage.] I'm not in the movement for self-sacrifice. [Get it? He signals his solidarity with the movement and his individuality.] I don't like that whole puritan idea. [Puritan is a copout word.] I'm in it for self-fulfillment. [Get it? He's on the same wave length as the kids.] If you've got any kind of self-consciousness [Now we are all worrying about his soul.] it seems to me, you realize you have all these elements in your life—a public voice, a private voice—and a lot of people find it upsetting to lead five different lives." [Two arms, two legs, and a head all nailed to the Cross, God have mercy on the poor man.] The students could not be expected to realize that this teacher was a faker in the confessional and should have been on his knees, that in a moral world God would have struck him dead for such mastery of the clichés. For he was busy sending out signals, not ideas, assuring the students that he wanted their love and that his mind was in the same mess as their own. Now, what was the original question?

This trivial example suggests the sinister and subtle power of the cliché as used today. The verbal man can use it to couch cowardice as a novel bravery, evasion as courageous confrontation, a blur in the head as profound philosophy. Universal education has rotated into the educational system thousands of people congested with received ideas, understanding only those clichés currently in fashion, signaling, signaling: love me, love me. When our universities are entirely filled with un-principled actors, we will really be in trouble, ready for a perfectly American version of the Fall of Ancient Rome. For this pathetic MIT professor had a perfect audience for the idea cliché: self-sacrifice, Puritan, self-fulfillment, self-consciousness, and then the anonymous escape into the vacuum, wrapped in self-consciousness.

The idea cliché, under the name of *idée reçue,* was systematized, but certainly not invented, in the last century by Gustave Flaubert. He compiled ideas that are passed around in certain groups, embodying the groups' accepted truths (or, sometimes, jokes). His difficulty, and ours, is that language is filled with old forgotten jokes that have turned into solid words in the dictionary; the jokes are now fossils. "Chauvinism," for example, derives from the surname of a Napoleonic veteran whose persistent raptures over Napoleon became a joke. The word became a synonym for another joke word "jingoism"; both are now used by some people as substitutes for "patriotism." But patriotism as an idea, meaning the preservation of an optimum habitat for the posterity, is an instinct that runs through the whole animal kingdom, excepting some modern men. It is no more a cliché than the law of gravity or a mammal's dependence on oxygen. The joke words, however, appear to make it a cliché, and try to tell us that we would be better off without it, or might even do without oxygen.

The present world is not unique in such foolishness, as can be seen in Flaubert's *Dictionary of Accepted Ideas*, written in French in the latter part of the nineteenth century, supposedly untranslatable but at last freely transposed to modern English by Jacques Barzun. His corruption of received ideas to accepted ideas may be construed as a further insult to the receiving mind.

These clichés are a hundred years old. Many entries, such as "KORAN. Book entirely about women, by Mohammed," are fairly meaningless today. Others, such as "HAM. Always from Mainz"; "LEATHER. It all comes from Russia"; "LEFTHANDED. Formidable fencers . . ." are inevitably obsolete. But in a skilled translation most are still intelligible, and many are still in use. Thus:

ANT. Model to cite in front of a spendthrift. Suggested the idea of savings banks.

ARISTOCRACY. Despise and envy it.

ATHEISTS. "A nation of atheists cannot survive."

BLONDES. Hotter than brunettes.

BRUNETTES. Hotter than blondes.

BUDGET. Never balanced.

CANNONADE. Affects the weather.

CATHOLICISM. Has had a good influence on art.

CAVALRY. Nobler than the infantry.

CHILDREN. Give signs of a passionate attachment to all children when others are looking on.

COMFORT. The most valuable discovery of modern times.

CONCESSIONS. Never make any. They ruined Louis XVI.

CONSPIRATORS. They feel a compulsion to write down their names on a list.

CORNS. Better than a barometer . . .

COUNTERFEITERS. Always work below ground.

DESCARTES. *Cogito ergo sum.*

EXCEPTION. Say it proves the rule, but don't venture to explain how.

EXTIRPATE. Verb applied only to heresy and corns.

GIRAFFE. Polite word to avoid calling a woman an old cow.

GLOVES. Confer respectability.

"GODDAM." The essence of the English language . . .

GUERRILLA. Does more harm to the enemy than the regular forces.

HOSTILITIES. Are like oysters, they have to be opened.

HYSTERIA. Confuse with nymphomania.

IDEALS. Perfectly useless.

INNOVATION. Always "dangerous."

LAWYERS. Too many in Parliament . . .

MAXIM. Never new; always consoling.

OPTIMIST. Synonym for imbecile.

POLICE. Always in the wrong.

PRUNES. Keep the bowels loose.

REGARDS. Always the best.

SIGH. Must be exhaled near a woman.

THUNDERBOLTS (FROM THE VATICAN). Laugh at them.

WORKMAN. Always honest—unless he is rioting.

Some of these must be truths, they have survived so well. Note these entries: budget, cannonade, comfort, corns, gloves, guerrilla, lawyers, police, prunes, workman. Barzun, the translator, ascribes all the clichés to a single group, the French bourgeoisie. He also believes that Flaubert had a total contempt for the users of the clichés. If we cannot understand that he is wrong on both counts, we cannot understand clichés. Flaubert, a handsome Norman of the Rouen area, saw both provincial society and such Parisians as Daudet, Zola, Turgenev, the Goncourts—that is, he gathered clichés at several levels. He knew very well that each group has its own clichés. And he must have known that clichés are only an attempt at simplified and usable thought; many are perfectly pardonable, and may even be valid.

Some reveal a man who is halfway well-informed. Barzun legitimately translates: "FLAMINGO. A bird, so called because native to Flanders." In English, this gives us a well-informed Frenchman who knows that the English name for the bird is flamingo, and that English dictionaries derive this word from Iberian for "Fleming," but does not happen to know that flamingoes do not come as far north as Belgium (except in zoos). However, the word for the scarlet bird comes from the Latin for "flame," and only by wild coincidence arrives at the same form as the Iberian Fleming.

But in French the cliché is very different. A stupid man had only confused *flamant*, French for "flamingo," with *flamand*, French for "Fleming." This will show that clichés do not travel well, whether from one language to another, one time to another, or one group to another. In a particular language, time, and group, every nuance and echo of the cliché is known to all. To define every inflection of the cliché might take a thousand words, but these words are never written.

A cliché expresses an arrested stage of a process of thought and information. It is a sort of fossil, a hardened vestige of what was once somewhat alive and real. The Rouen Frenchman had seen *flamands*, but he had only heard of *flamants*. He consolidated these experiences into a single fossil structure: both are native to Flanders, thus closing up a gap in his knowledge.

Nevertheless, to despise him would be smug and unbecoming. In a parvenu world, where nearly everybody is on the way up, one will hear many clichés as bad as the Flemish flamingo, and one had better suppress the hauteur. Of the same kind, and in civilized company, is a recent one that Hungarians shake hands with the left hand. This was tracked to a phrase in a William Styron novel. The sentence ran: ". . . who, extending for some reason his left hand instead of right, like a Hungarian, gave my palm a squeeze . . ." Writers should be more careful. This sentence can be read as saying that Hungarians prefer to shake hands with the left hand.

Many clichés are born as errors, and often not so innocent errors, such as Lenin's invention that the only significant man is the proletarian. The Chinese were long offended, and justly, by the cliché falsehood about their women. Some Russians today may be offended by Lenin's law that they are all peasants or workers. As a harmless example, *Eminence Grise* now means Cardinal Richelieu, but it doesn't; it refers to Richelieu's secretary, Father Joseph.

In America at this minute we must admit that we can define the clichés of only one country, America, of only one language, English, and of only one time, 1970. Even beyond these limitations, one had better confess that one really understands only the clichés of one's own group, within that place, language, and period.

In America the most accessible cliché groups are the audiences of the mass media. As we inspect the media in the following pages, we will discover that various groups are at war with one another. These antitheses reconfirm the truth that a cliché must be allocated to its particular group, and may outrage another group.

❧ 2 ❧

Fact or Happening

There burst on the lethargic journalism of Calvin Coolidge's world in 1923 the clenched, running prose of *Time* magazine. This purported to say as quickly as possible everything a week's newspapers said; it thus satirized newspapers, and should in theory have destroyed them.

The thirties were enraged by such entries (June 12, 1933) as: "ENGAGED. Alfonso, 26, Prince of Asturias, eldest son of Alfonso XIII and heir claimant to the Spanish throne, and Señorita Edelmira Sampedro, 27, daughter of a Cuban merchant. . . . In the face of his father's bitter opposition to the match, the Prince was quoted: 'I love her and want to marry her. Let Juan have the throne.'" The rage was caused by the authoritarian tone, the spelling of Alphonso, and the suspicion that the editors had invented Alphonso's statement.

And so, throughout the thirties, everybody proceeded to imitate *Time*'s style in various relatively limp versions. At least an authoritative factualism swept American media. The most pitiful expressions of this are "Surveys show . . ." and "Experts find . . ." Based on unspecified and unarguable researches and statistics, simplified points are made by *Reader's Digest, Pageant, Coronet, et al.,* and with a more sophisticated deliberation, by *Look* and others. The Time Inc. approach is accepted as a consensus. But it should be noted that early *Time* style was a pious and even fanatic canon, enforced by the terror of making a mistake, as if there were a Torquemada in the wings, as indeed there was.

In this same period, a wildly contrary style flounced along as if *Time* had never been invented. Cozening, allusive, narcissistic, it serenaded its own audience like an hysterical Circe, unmoved by *Time*'s gutturals. This will be identified in due course.

Time has changed, it is true. As of the issue of April 5, 1968, whose only distinction is that it was the current issue when I reached this point, we find the following ideas or clichés:

The Vietnam *Tet* offensive of early 1968 was a military failure, a political success.

Bombing North Vietnam is effective.

That war is at the stage of the American Civil War just before Grant took command.

Nixon at least knows the questions. He is not a conservative.

Doctor King in Memphis was exploited by the black hoodlums.

A sure sign of democracy (*vide* Czechoslovakia) is nude movies.

"The taste of blood" (Israel) "is not easily forgotten."
Indonesian politicians are still thieves.
Mia Farrow Sinatra is still a silly girl.
Capital, if not capitalism, still rules the world.
Judaic scholarship is a hot item, academically.
The press loathes Bobby Kennedy.
Yippies are ecstatic people.
College teachers are unmotivated careerists.
Integrated education works, if there are talented
teachers and foundation funds.
The First Amendment does not give any right to riot.
Dada is great.
High interest rates are bad.
Sell strawberry shortcake before showing meat and
potatoes.
The best approach to reality is "in a slightly joky
way."
"The greatest good for the greatest number" might
appear to justify gang-rape.
Whites can understand blacks better by jumping
around more, like blacks.
The old Time Inc. spirit survives but "in a slightly
joky way," trying to have opinions on Mia Farrow,
yippies, and rape, and jumping around more. And
remember the date, for all statements are legitimately
stamped with a date. The issue appeared just before
the murder of Doctor Martin Luther King, Jr., which
was at once vulgarized into the cliché: "Whitey kills
blacks," when in fact one Southern white had killed
one Southern black. The blacks opened a violence that
might have produced results for Lenin, Mussolini, or
Hitler in a cabinet system of government, but under
the American system exploded in a vacuum, not in the

South but, if historians will believe it, in the North, which had befriended and subsidized the Negroes expelled from the bankrupt Southern plantations since the Civil War. (And what was that war all about?)

The subsequent assassination of Robert Kennedy also made obsolete everything said about him in this issue.

The *Time* clichés today, unlike those of my own day there, are fairly modest and perhaps embarrassed. *Time* does not seem quite sure of itself. Anyone skeptical of the listed ideas is invited to read that issue from cover to cover.

The complete antithesis of *Time* and its imitators is the group of magazines paced by *Vogue* and *Harper's Bazaar*. This audience does not want to read and think; it wants to feel and dream. Hence, the editors must put the reader into a transport of delight in three or four words.

Thus in the *Vogue* of April 1, 1968, we find: "Smouldering black jet and glistery black braid"; "Green grow the ruffles—vivid voile fluttering down"; "asymmetric bareness"; "tawny tapering rib cage"; "subtle beat of flower ways"; "the sound of ylang and myrrh, of patchouli, spices and sandalwood"; "princess of some mythic tribe . . . the most delicious sort of fakery"; "to hear her say 'Philadelphia' is like listening to a wood thrush at evening."

The wood thrush actually sings only three notes, and couldn't get any further than "delph." But in *Vogue* facts are inconsequential; what is important is the intention of flattering ignorant adorables. The style is a delicious parody of beautiful English and calls for real editorial talent.

The ideas in the April 1, 1968, issue are:

The most important thing in the world is your skin. No, it's your eyes. No, it's your smell. No, it's your hair.

The new color this week is green.

Making a movie of *Romeo and Juliet* is a ball, complete with actors "scratching their codpieces."

"The most beautiful beauty training camp in the world. . . . Make the skin fit better . . . fresh young glow." Facial masks of "strawberries, mangoes, avocados, cucumbers, papayas, usually mixed with honey." Mexican servants with "beautiful hair and fine teeth."

An egg of "ambrosial, spring dew" emulsion.

In Texas, restaurants "spill out" along a river "edged with dripping bougainvillaea." Dallas: "skyscrapers rising like spun glass."

Turtle oil "stings not, smooths yes."

Bill Cosby is not sufficiently pro-Negro.

A girl must Happen—"shining, shimmering, flashing, smouldering." "To live today is big time or else you are a blank."

Texas is where it's happening. The semi-desert supports "elegance and sophistication." (This about people who are ravishing the land, the fauna, and the water table.) Money, money, money.

One's life must be a Happening, "or else you are a blank." Reality appears, but it is better than real; it is "spring dew," which has peculiar properties not shared by dew at any other time. Strawberries and honey are best applied externally.

Just in case *Vogue* was running a high fever that issue, try another, November 1, 1967, and the delirium is the same: "The crash of velvet, left; it's cymbalic"; "Black velvet at its most fatale . . ."; ". . . falls like a liquid-gold love note against the calf"; "sumptuous and innocent like the young Edward in a Holbein portrait"; "great glossy, luxurious fluff of fur"; "actor with a sonar feeling for the meanings under words." While the words just miss meaning anything, we get the image of a somewhat hard, realistic, idly cultivated lady, but a lady so indubitable that she can afford to use such slang as "the works" and notice actors scratching their codpieces. The cryptology about "the meanings under words" reminds us that under *Vogue's* words is the well-understood cliché that the reader can escape from the miserable facts of herself into something cymbalic, fatale, sumptuous, glossy, luxurious, and into still other adjectives in the next issue. The magazines did not invent and impose this idea; the ladies invented it. The magazines are only accommodating them.

The magazines urge a heightened narcissism in which one detects a tone of aggression. This is not the old femininity. This girl is Happening; she is "big time."

Since Time Inc. hardly notices *Vogue-Harper's Bazaar* (I have, perhaps, because I have worked for all three companies), one may ask why these two styles have been bracketed here. A sufficient reason is that the current high style, both in and out of magazines, is a theoretically impossible combination of just these two idioms.

Since the proportions of the recipe vary with every story or book, no names will be given. We find the Time Inc. factualism in the details of materials, brands, gun calibers, horsepowers, carburetors, tailors, resorts, hotels, restaurants, etc. This gives an air of nonfiction. But the facts are embedded in a relatively high-pitched, whirling, psychedelic style which, as in the fashion magazines, tries to catch the actual sensation of feeling, smelling, showing off, being admired or, rather, adored. The style, however, overpowers the facts. The latter become incidental, as if "thrown away."

The style, like that of the fashion magazines, is aggressively narcissistic or exhibitionistic. The cliché is "I am beautiful," complete with every bodily function shared by all the more than three billion people now in the world. And so this writing bears down on the obscenities which are so inevitable and unremarkable. Perhaps "eat" too should be an obscenity, for anyone who eats is about to be obscene, if he or she is narcissistic or exhibitionistic. In the *Vogue* issue the actors "scratching their codpieces" should have been such a signal or cliché.

The point of high-style writing is that you, the ordinary reader, are hopelessly outside the important life of the times. Your disability may simply be that you are *not* a child or homosexual or Negro or idle rich. Or you may feel not quite up to acquiring the motorcycle and tattoos, or the LSD, or flying to a Mexican beauty farm, or not eating your strawberries and avocado, or tightening your forehead skin with invisible tape, or surfing or sky-diving, or learning how to kill people with your bare hands. Of course *The Song of Roland* and *Idylls of the King* also excluded the reader, but through no fault of his own, only by an accident of time and birth. The modern exclusion reveals to the reader his own failure of nerve.

Vogue tries to convey that it is "where it's happening." Time Inc. cannot afford to exclude readers. It watches "where it's happening," but is clearly not at the party. In a development that in the thirties would have seemed monstrously impossible, *Vogue* style has infiltrated Time Inc. *Vogue* has won the battle. *Vogue,* the Delilah, has cut the hair of the former Samson, Time Inc.

In the April 1 *Time*, we see yippies, gang rape, Negroes, "jumping around," and a movie review parody of hillbilly talk. *Life* has captioned a picture story with translated Hindu poetry and (August 12, 1967) printed the metaphors "The music . . . can sound like a cascade of spilled golden nails"; and "Her incredible 6-foot-4 frame, collapsible like a spider and extensible to a sexy derrick."

This is a flat abandonment of the Time Inc. system. I have never heard golden nails spilling, but I am certain the sound is not at all musical. A Time Inc. checker in the old days had to know. If she had verified that, she would have been fired, an hour after the writer had slunk into the night. And can spiders be described as collapsible or derricks as sexy? No.

The old Time Inc. said that matters are exactly as they are, no more, no less, sometimes in areas where matters were not that clear. The effort, in my opinion, was worthy, if not always successful. It would still be worthy, but today it would not be chic. The new-shorn Samson can only watch the party through a clouded window.

And that is the grand cliché today: Where is the party? Where is it happening? Once the question referred to Negroes; now it applies to children who have appropriated the Negro style. The idea that children know something special (as if no adult had ever been a child) is the terrified obsession of some editors. Their constant worry is: What are these flocks of chickadees up to now? In fact I have never heard of a modern juvenile lunacy that was not antedated by my friends and myself some forty years ago, except that we had some instinct for survival and self-respect. The trouble with having such adults as editors is that they like to pretend that they were never children.

But the answer to "Where is it happening?" might be: A thousand miles up the Orinoco River to the villages of the handsome, proud, muscular, naked Guaica Indians, the only tribe not dying out but increasing. The men wage war, catch huge river turtles, make poisons and fine arrows. They use the yogo drug and consume the ashes of their dead. They have a wonderful diet, including thirty-eight kinds of fruit. Whatever the men do they do to excess, until exhaustion, and then they will rest for days. Some are called "Shrieking Monkeys." Guaicas make all other Happenings ridiculous.

⤜§ 3 §⤴

Group Therapy or
Pointlessness

Another conflict, fully as desperate as the foregoing,
rages behind the bland covers on the magazine stands.

On one side are what can be called the tutelary
or prescriptive magazines—*Reader's Digest, Pageant,
Coronet*, etc.—which function as your lawyer, doctor,
dentist, tax accountant, psychiatrist, travel agent, and
so on. Obviously they want to help, and they do it by
discovering truths that apply roughly to the whole
audience, that is, necessarily, clichés. They are as
anxious as Karl Marx to save the world and, like him,
expose the grave difficulties of the mass solution.

Group Therapy, as this is called, is probably inevitable in a large, crowded society. Where people
are very numerous and therefore relatively valueless,
personal solutions and individual cures begin to look
absurdly expensive, wasteful, and inefficient. We would
like to have a rich variety of independently developed

people, just as we would like to have a rich organic
soil. But just as we desperately dump inorganic chem-
icals into the tired soil, we organize Alcoholics Anonymous, Gamblers Anonymous, group clinics, reducing
courses, judo schools, and so on to keep the huge, tired
society going at all.

Official Group Therapies include labor unions, political organizations, and colleges which are, among other
things, agencies for imposing *idées reçues*. A strike or a
protest march or a football game is also Group Therapy,
taking a problem, a dialogue, and producing a mass
solution, good or bad. In these three cases, the *idées
reçues* are no joke; dissent is not tolerated by the faithful. Alcoholics Anonymous, I am told, thrives on contrary opinions. The ultimate lesson of Group Therapy,
however, is that no individual is unique; he is more
like everybody else than he is different from them.
In case of neurosis or tragedy, this can be consoling
news. But this truth has its sinister side. With the
labor union it is as with the three musketeers: all for
one, and the one had better be for all.

Reader's Digest is the classic vendor of Group Therapy, with the best imaginable will. A survey of a year's
issues would undoubtedly turn up every kind and
decent cliché offered the American people, for their
indubitable benefit. Every piece in this magazine has
a clear and simple point, which is further condensed
in the title, which is then printed on the cover to attract
the attention of people who may desperately need the
cliché.

Reader's Digest condenses itself. Therefore, the intention here is to drop to a lower and more amateurish
level of Group Therapy as seen in *Pageant*. This mag-

azine gives the effect of cleaning up behind *Reader's Digest,* rather than concentrating on the reader's life problems.

In the May 1968 issue of *Pageant* we find:

Only Presidents with charm (not Johnson) can afford to be losers.

McCarthy is the eggheads' candidate; Wallace the Neanderthals'.

Actors: Rod Steiger, brutal sensualist, likes to annoy women by tearing up money. Dame Edith Evans, seventy-nine, alone but not lonely, did not live with Bernard Shaw. Faye Dunaway likes fame, money, brass beds.

Nobody is on time.

New laws on processed meat still permit rotten frankfurters.

Christ did not believe in the consumer economy.

Transplantable hearts are a new national resource, subject to the law of supply and demand.

Raccoons are charming busybodies.

It's nice for boys and girls to meet.

American garbage is a mounting nightmare.

Psycho-sex tests of schoolchildren are a criminal impudence.

Take it easy buying a country place—finally, nirvana.

Not all relationships are necessarily sexual.

Divorces are often funny.

Prenatal exercises can make childbirth nearly painless.

The right words can sometimes win a girl.

The worst job in sports is the hockey goalkeeper's.

The magazine is working hard to make clear, simple points, some of them useful to the reader. *Reader's Digest* works even harder, as if it were alone responsible for the health of the whole society. Every issue says "Life is good," "Everybody is pretty decent," "Modern medicine is miraculous." Its kindness and concern are clear even when it makes points that are the opposite of the general truth. For example, utility companies' stubborn fight to keep from putting transmission lines underground is well-known to the Federal Power Commission. However, the *Digest* (November 1967) says in effect that there are utilities that *like* to put their lines underground. This may be read as suggesting please, everybody, be nice. It may work. In the same issue are pieces saying that local citizens can actually influence highway commissions, very few kids use drugs, and the Viet Cong don't really want to fight. These may discourage highway commissions and drug peddlers, but probably not the Viet Cong.

These hardworking, highminded magazines have a deadly foe that may be more influential than them all, and undo all their splendid work. This would be *The New Yorker*.

The philosophy of this magazine is enigmatic. One gathers it knows exactly what it is doing, but it is not easy to see quite what that is.

The New Yorker's present character is improbably derived from the success of a kind of very brief short story contributed around 1930 by a struggling writer, John O'Hara, and slipped into the back of the book. The dazzling novelty of this genre was that the story had no point, and numerous other writers discovered that they too could produce this sort of thing without effort. With these stories, the reader was at perfect liberty to supply any point he liked, or murmur helplessly, "Life!" And then, mysteriously, the genre vanished from view and has never, so far as I know, re-appeared.

The magazine at this point was still fighting for its life. It is evident that the editor, Harold Ross, suddenly saw that he had been given his formula for the whole magazine, and preferred to keep it a secret. The philosophy he took from the pointless stories was simple enough: There is no point to anything. (Remember, this was at the beginning of the Depression, and at the end of Prohibition. And remember that Ross was a cunning hick from the Rocky Mountain plateau.)

Today the primitivism of the philosophy is masked by a sophisticated literacy. But for all the well-chosen words, nothing ever gets added up or summarized or comes to a head, to produce a workable point. If you ask a *New Yorker* editor how many apples he has, he will not answer "Ten," but instead, "Five and three and two," and then explain how he got them, when, in what order, from whom, what kinds they are, and something about the history of apples. He will insist that it would be incorrect to say ten apples, because his apples are not all exactly the same. The aborigine Guaica from the Orinoco headwaters would understand him perfectly.

Since anybody's average day is fairly pointless and indecisive (Waterloos, Pearl Harbors, and November 22, 1963, are infrequent), or if it has a point we do not recognize it, the pointless world of *The New Yorker* has a peculiar and winning familiarity. It is even rather interesting. It does not burden us with all that good advice and pointed information in the *Reader's Digest*. Insensibly, the reader comes to feel that he does not need any advice while he is reading *The New Yorker*.

For this hour the real world is a zoo, and he is outside looking in at the specimens who read the *Reader's Digest*. Renew your subscription.

To be both pointless and interesting is a highly skilled operation. A long piece on fishing in Connecticut was both; a longer piece on lawns was only the former. In the immediate issue I picked up, April 6, 1968, the main piece might be construed as having an oblique and futuristic point. *The New Yorker's* superb art is to blunt, bend, and bury it. The idea is that there is a man who has learned how to live off the wild plants in field, forest, and park. This might be useful knowledge, in case of atomic holocaust, for the survivors. Such a point, literally offered to the reader as a helpful service for the end of the world, would of course sound like monstrous satire. Most editors would be horrified. But in the world of the pointless, nothing is taboo. *The New Yorker* story simply sticks to an hour-by-hour diary of a foraging trip and the picaresque memories of the botanist-gourmet. There is no point.

In this issue a pointless roundup of election campaign activity lingers on details of a game of checkers and the fact that elsewhere the chairs were "of the folding type, but had imitation-leather cushions and armrests." This apparently shameless padding is in fact working hard, for its function is to lose any possible point in the recitation. This procedure makes the editors' preference in candidates (obviously, the last one in the sequence) almost invisible and, in fact, sneaky. The pose of perfect innocence, perfected by *The New Yorker*, must inevitably, given the nature of man, be corrupted into winning the argument by appearing not to argue. *The New Yorker's* propaganda is subliminal, that is, the ultimate wickedness.

Amusingly, because the coincidence is ex post facto, the mathematical metaphor given above (concerning the ten apples) is literally the theme of this issue's cover cartoon: a scholarly seal thinking of an equation showing with mathematical signs that little fish turn into big fish. The cover makes this a ridiculous proposition. (I can already hear *The New Yorker*'s explanation of what the cover really means. Yeah, yeah.)

Since the proof of the pointlessness is in every pudding, I need not continue.

The fable of the Emperor's Clothes must have attracted the late Harold Ross. But instead of becoming the seeing child on the sidewalk, he brilliantly chose to make his magazine the foolish Emperor with his exquisite, expensive clothes which were far superior to the crass point of covering his nakedness but elevated the pride of the bystanders who believed in them. Nothing, unfortunately, is always superior to something.

The intellectual status of *The New Yorker* has continued because pointlessness is perfectly adaptable to existentialism, nihilism, socialism, pacifism, McLuhanism, psychedelism, structuralism, anything, whereas other magazines, confronted with novelties, are obliged to think hard, make a conclusion, and express a point. Pointlessness has no such necessities. *The New Yorker* might seem to be expressed by the mathematical sign zero, originally borrowed from India, the archetype nation of pointlessness. Certainly the zero, put after any reality, does something quite magical. India had invented something really important.

As with Time Inc. and *Vogue*, we must seek the victor as between *Reader's Digest et al.* and *The New Yorker*. The latter addresses America's middlebrows,

the key people in the society. When these people, faced
with real problems—bosses, subordinates, wives, children—see themselves as pointless characters in a *New
Yorker* story, article, or cartoon, they give up. In the
pleasantest way imaginable, they have been emascu-
lated, depersonalized, unpolarized, disoriented. (Alienated!)

The *New Yorker* message, or cliché, that everything
is created equal, that is, equally nonsignificant, erodes
the bases of the *Reader's Digest*'s positives or points,
and must in the long run be pronounced the winning
side. The present visible condition of the society con-
firms the award.

Furthermore, we can see pointlessness infiltrating
the point magazines. The *Pageant* issue has several
such pieces: on actors, raccoons, boys and girls, funny
divorces, etc.

The philosophy of pointlessness must have some nu-
trition, for apart from the magazine's good circulation
and relatively high advertising rates, very few *New
Yorker* editors have committed suicide. Nor do I mean
to criticize them for this. The entrenched confidence
that "We don't know anything but we're infallible"
must have some psychic power, some inner fortifica-
tion which I can only envy. Good pay probably helps
too. Incidentally, this magazine is said to have the
world's largest inventory of unused writing and car-
toons.

The final revelation of *The New Yorker* would lie in
its rejects. John Cheever, an established *New Yorker*
writer, unexpectedly has a story (inferentially rejected
by *The New Yorker*) in the January 1968 *Playboy*.

It is a beautiful story. Why was it rejected? But of course; it has a point, a happy ending, and several clearly signaled morals. It would have been all wrong in *The New Yorker*, though most people would be hard put to explain why.

Esquire addresses much the same audience as *The New Yorker* while trying much harder to be *avant-garde*. It has a confirmed habit of playing practical jokes on its readers. After a few of these, the fearful reader doesn't believe anything he sees in *Esquire*, and so may receive a painful version of *The New Yorker*'s pointlessness. As the reader's ego and superego fight for survival, he is intellectually hardened. Ultimately he may be able to stay one jump ahead of the editors. *Esquire* teaches another truth about life: Everybody may be lying to you and, from time to time, probably is. This is calculated to instill a healthy paranoia.

Esquire, May 1968, had the following to say:

The printed word is still useful.

Bob Dylan (records) is still the master. The Stones and Donovan are suspect.

Norman Mailer can't end sentences, says Dwight MacDonald, who can't help the fact that he's always right.

Champion golfers hate tournaments.

Heretics are the most amusing people; but not pornographers.

Watch Conductor Daniell Revenaugh (if you can find him).

Travel editor foams on restrictions against travel and travel editors.

Movies are more grisly than funny.

Richard Nixon is a joyless, hardworking parvenu,

hoist into celebrity on the crucifix of Alger Hiss. All his bangs come out whimpers but don't play poker or war games with him.

Joke: Six Presidential candidates are shown with hair re-styling that turns them into store mannequins and would ruin them. Women, who take hair seriously, were bewildered by this.

Joke: Supposed photographic blunders by the editors.

Boggy story: Writers are bad news for young girls.

Parody montage of a Breughel painting with modern faces dubbed in. It means anything you want.

Biography of the murdered hippie Groovy Hutchinson.

Notice of *Time*'s criticism of *Time* (actually a *Time* joke).

With illustration of girl leaping bicycle over Buchenwald gravestones, story of a German loner who plots to rape and kill a sixteen-year-old but doesn't get around to it. Therefore, a joke.

Negro musicians love Europe, especially Paris and Scandinavia.

White dinner jackets must be a little different.

Dirty books are as legitimate as *Life* magazine. (Money.) Interviewers of authors generally haven't read the book.

The classic cocktails of 1934 have deteriorated.

Travel editor saves money on travel: Group Inclusive Tours.

Thirty days without a bath can literally decay you.

Supposed Negro rapist may have been welcomed by white girl.

John Wayne's son: "When you're making a picture, the Indians are the bad guys." Joke.

Stereo is getting better.

Seersucker suits are better.

Men's clothes are better (but odder). Add straw hats, colored shoes, colored cuff links. No jokes here.

As in *The New Yorker*, the contents flatter the reader that he has no problems and can afford to dawdle over esoterica. It is true that *Esquire* does not quite reach *The New Yorker*'s Tibetan plateau of pointlessness. Still the material listed is fairly useless; the readers certainly don't need to be told to bathe. As esoterica, the contents are not spectacular. An essential part of the recipe, as it was forty years ago, is something about Negroes; to which has been added something about children. There is remarkably little notice of European culture, as compared with the pre-World War II sophistication. Europe is now only a resort.

Parallel to the gleeful notice of *Time*'s criticizing itself, *Esquire* runs a very bad review of *Report from Iron Mountain,* part of which had previously been printed in *Esquire.* To repudiate oneself is supposed to indicate a bad character, or perhaps no character. If these editors truly, naïvely, believe in anything, it is the last thing they are going to admit. And yet they probably do believe in seersucker suits and colored cuff links.

The New Yorker pointlessness, however, has affected the tone and vocabulary of other magazines, primarily those read by rattled WASPs. In *Architectural Forum* the key adverb is "nicely." The trees have grown nicely.

Things turned out nicely. To anyone who thought that a magazine page was a chance to say something, the word "nicely" is abject surrender. The writer just wants to get off the page. "Nicely," of course.

Similarly in *Harper's* (November 1968) we find the sentences "The next big town on the way west across New York State is Utica, then comes Syracuse, and if you persist you will eventually arrive in Buffalo"; *"Finian's Rainbow* was one of the sweetest musical comedies ever to reach Broadway"; "jump like he'd seen a snake"; "cities in the process of pulling up their socks." This language has the great virtue of leaving the mind almost instantly, leaving no trace. It is therefore pointless. If one heard such snatches at a cocktail party, one would move on.

These were the *Harper's* staff writers. The great blob of foreign material in the issue, as in *The New Yorker*, does not define the magazine. In this case it was Norman Mailer's phantasmagoria of the Republican and Democratic conventions in 1968, in a blending of the Time Inc. and *Vogue* styles. For the Republicans, he concentrates on the WASPs. For the Democrats, he moves from amateur psychoanalysis to Knute Rockne pep talks in the locker room to lovemaking to horror stories, and now and then drops to his knees in the confessional. The performance is interesting but it compounds the bedlam. The person of the writer blots out the great historical event. When the gas blows away, only Mailer is visible, and even he through a glass darkly.

Harper's also offers the WASPs a version of the familiar pun-anagram crossword puzzle, with the additional clues of an acrostic. Speaking as a WASP, I was insulted by its childishness, even without using the acrostic clues. The genteel pose just now is to be stupid and unaffected, and listen attentively to children, but I must tell *Harper's* that the WASPs are not quite that stupid; it is only a pose. The crossword puzzle is therefore pointless. Mailer's tirade is ultimately pointless, for it advised against voting at all in 1968. The WASP is left, as in *The New Yorker*, in the air.

A pointless world has the strange effect of welcoming the ranter. One delusion today is that every ranter is Saint Paul. But Saint Paul had something to say, which he corrupted. These ranters have only their own glands. In the pointless void of *The New Yorker*, any loud outcry is permissible if it is pointless, a scream in the dark, to which nobody pays any attention.

The New Yorker pointlessness often reaches heights that are satires on itself, as in a story of a woman who regarded a picture of an octopus making love to a dead woman floating in the ocean as the perfect quintessence of sexuality. Surely this was the near-perfection of pointlessness or futility, only to be surpassed by the wooing of a corpse by a sea anemone, starfish, or segmented worm, which are hermaphrodites. An octopus could theoretically do it. The whole idea derives from an old joke.

The pointlessness of the original O'Hara stories in *The New Yorker* almost thirty years ago was duplicated in a story in the *Harper's* issue examined. A prize should have been offered the reader who had the most plausible theory as to the writer's message; but it would have been a ten-way tie. A comment on the attitude toward the WASP is that both *The New Yorker* and *Harper's* live on liquor advertising.

❧ 4 ❧

Pain or Pleasure

A shaking and pitiful conflict divides two other groups of magazines, that is, audiences. The operative clichés are that pain is for women, pleasure for men.

The prototype of the women's magazines is *Ladies' Home Journal* which, unlike *Vogue* and *Harper's Bazaar*, really talks to the American woman and makes hardly any effort to be part of "what's happening." For its purposes it knows what's happening: 100 million females. Parenthetically, it runs a middlebrow column called "What's Happening."

The issue of March 1968 is loaded with pain. The fixture "Can This Marriage Be Saved?" tells the story of a handsome swinger who gambled away all the savings of his young air stewardess wife. Next, we learn that children, ignorant of the Bible, cannot finish the sentence "Pride goeth before a ————." "Medicine Today" is more bad news. "It's in Your Mind" is still more—for example, family fights give the man ulcers and the woman arthritis, never the reverse. Women can love two men at once, however. Then we are told in a symposium that parents who spank and apologize produce dropout, runaway children, or hippies. Then come two unexpected jokes: horoscopes for dogs and shoppers. Next come manners and finance, both painful. Then a change of pace—luxurious bathrooms. But hard reality resumes: twenty-five part-time jobs for women.

The pain continues in the body of the magazine. A respectable, handsome young Negro teacher is accused by a female white pupil of having tried to make love to her. The town "honkies" rally to his defense; the girl is routed and ostracized.

But virtue does not always have such a hard time, and so we are given the women's favorite TV personality and his new chateau; an hospitable millionaire yachtsman and his guests; and three working wives modeling clothes for home and office. Then a collection of curlyheads with directions: "Careful plotting and planning of each little ringlet. . . . For fat sausage curls, use rollers. . . . Wind on end papers for the neatest finish. For tiny tendrils, use clips." Then some flower-patterned dresses. Then how to make soufflés—an agonizing ordeal, fraught with failure—opening twelve pages of recipes, diets, and cooking hints. Finally, a painful novel by Simone de Beauvoir, balanced by a pleasant trip to Holland.

Significantly, the editors have realized that pain and fear rack their readers, and had conducted a poll on the paramount fears. In this issue, the results are announced: (1) hate and killing; (2) fat; (3) money management; (4) what young people are thinking; (5) irreligious children; (6) lack of willpower; (7) inability to stop smoking.

All seven are defeatist fears. For these ladies, most of the hate and killing is far away; fat is the corollary to happy eating; comfort costs money; the young aren't very good at thinking; God can take care of Himself; and the last two are just pretty apologies. The *Journal* called in a psychiatrist who made bold to name three fears the ladies ought to have but hadn't mentioned: promiscuous daughters, homosexual sons, and alcohol. The ladies deserve credit for not having slandered their families or degraded themselves. But all seven of the avowed fears are clichés, in that they had been fossilized in conversations among the ladies, and become successful signals of respectability. The voiced fear that one's daughter was promiscuous or one's son was a homosexual would not get anyone into a suburban country club. A degree of alcoholism is a distinction, not a scandal, in many groups, though this rule is going out of fashion. The conventional fears in other times would have been a drunken son and a spinster daughter, as in the Brontë family, but these fears could have been avowed without loss of status. They were well-fossilized clichés. The dissolute daughter and the sodomite son have certainly broken loose from the family. They may be chic, but they are not conversational clichés. In an odd way these children have lowered themselves from persons into things. The parents of things may very well have nightmares. Whether nightmares can be clichés I cannot say.

This whole subject is painful.

But there is a brighter world where all these anxieties

are comical and only pleasure reigns. Here is a princely somebody who wants to leap on the lady who has spent so many hours arranging her careful ringlets and, dispelling all her fears, rumple her coiffure and tumble her into bed. Of course, against every *Journal* stricture, she is complaisant, for this has always been her delicious destiny. The tiny ringlets scrupulously prepared with clips had no higher purpose than to enflame the conquering virility of this centaur. When he has had his will, presumably, she must go home and begin again plotting and planning the "fat sausage curls."

The official philosophy of *Playboy* is the inspired, self-evident cliché "Pleasure is better than pain." The pleasure is signaled in every issue by numbers of jubilant breasts and buttocks. These are presumed to convince us that pain has been abolished. If pain is synonymous with effort or work, one might well reply, "Pain is better than pleasure," precisely because it earns pleasure. If one had spent a few months getting to know the ladies who own these irreproachable bosoms and bottoms, they would really mean something. Such effort, or work, should not be neglected. There is an ancient and traditional word for the sequence "Pleasure now; pay later." The word is hell. It is still operative.

The publisher is primarily interested in the pictures rather than in the text; perhaps in consequence, the latter is at a very high level. A synopsis of a particular issue would mean little, since most of the text is fiction, weighted toward fantasy and nightmare, sometimes in the literal meaning of incubus. These stories increasingly admit the uses of tenderness toward the female, and even respect. Centaurs still appear in *Playboy* car-toons, but less often in the text. The idea is still that the girl will bring the man breakfast in bed, but it is suggested that a little consideration will make the compliance more probable. The magazine, it should be noted, is not even skirting the salacious; it is more properly described by the old-fashioned word risqué.

The clichés are so integral that they are nearly nominal, ritual rehearsals of a doctrine that is understood to be a quaint game:

Girls love to be kissed.

Men are, per se, fascinating to women.

The masterful (but now also clever) man can have anybody he wants.

It is better to be rich.

Staying up all night is exciting.

Visually, the moment of truth is the female nipple.

A little sadism is a good idea.

High-speed cars are great.

Very big businessmen are wise and good.

Babies are not a factor.

Much of *Playboy* is on a higher literary level than, for example, *Esquire*, but the total impression is constricted by the contextual assumption: A new girl; she likes me; wow! Everyone knows that generally this is a delicate, subjective, and uncommon situation that cannot very well be mass-reproduced, and certainly not every month. A hardworking *Playboy* would give much of its space to explaining the human female to young men; that is, it would duplicate much of the *Ladies' Home Journal*. The January 1968 issue includes in fact a piece on "The New Girl," who proposes to be not "an appendage on some man but her own unique self." A revised version could have appeared in the

Journal. In short, *Playboy* is taking a second look at pain.

In this war of clichés, the *Ladies' Home Journal* would seem to be eroding, ever so faintly, the *Playboy* philosophy. The ladies' fears appear more valid than the young men's joys.

❧ 5 ❧

Seven Group Clichés

Granted that one person may read two or more magazines, he roughly accepts the ideas in the magazines he reads. These become his *idées reçues,* but may be repellent or mystifying to the nonreader, who has collected different clichés.

The audiences described here divide crudely into two sets. One set reads for necessity, the other as a luxury. The role of problem-solver is assumed by *Time,* the digests (*Reader's Digest, Pageant, Coronet*) and the women's magazines (*Ladies' Home Journal et al.*). A world essentially without problems is represented by *Vogue, Harper's Bazaar, The New Yorker, Esquire,* and *Playboy.*

The mottoes of the first group are, respectively, "Life is facts," "Life is earnest," and "Life is pain"; and of the second group, "Life is whee!," "Life is pointless," "Life is lies," and "Life is pleasure."

These would seem to be deadly enemies but they coexist very easily. The *Ladies' Home Journal* reader may quite possibly read also *Vogue* or *Time* or *The New Yorker*, or even all four, without any serious schizophrenia. Pain, whee, facts, and pointlessness would all swirl together in her head. She would therefore have four cliché vocabularies in her repertory, and would use each with the appropriate company, just as Flaubert learned the difference between Rouen society and Paris society. Nonetheless, the pain and the whee! would tend to cancel each other out, and the pointlessness would blunt the facts.

There are some correspondences among the groups. Negroes are championed by *Vogue, Esquire,* and *Ladies' Home Journal,* criticized by *Time.* Children are defended by *Time, Vogue, Pageant, Esquire, Ladies' Home Journal,* criticized by *Esquire* and *Ladies' Home Journal.* It is conspicuous that *Playboy* does not notice the grimy contentions of life, except those of racing drivers, billionaires, and lovers.

Heroism, which is sometimes defined as the American ideal, finds a voice in *Time, Vogue,* occasionally the digests, rarely *Esquire, Playboy,* but not in *The New Yorker* or *Ladies' Home Journal.*

It is clear that from these varied sources no single unanimous set of American clichés can possibly be excerpted. What can be done is to define the magazine philosophies briefly.

Time: The truth about an event can be described quite briefly the very week it happened. Because conflict is the only interesting subject (true), war is not all bad. Republicans are better. Democracy is less decadent than the backward nations. The proper use of money is power. Power is a wonderful thing. But still it would be lovely to be at that party "where it's happening."

Vogue: We are the party. Flattery is better than bread; adjectives are the medium; superlatives are the minimum. Happiness is for sale; bring money. When strawberries, avocados, and honey can be lathered on the face, it would be silly to eat them. Rich people are beautiful. Looking rich is nearly as beautiful. Being beautiful is, however, as demanding as playing middle linebacker in pro football.

The digests: Every problem has an answer. Every difficulty has an explanation. Every disaster has a silver lining. The world is really quite nice. Modern science is omniscient and miraculous. An expert or a survey or a "study" invariably produces absolute truth. Most of the world's leaders are thoroughly nice people. Wild animals are fascinating. There are still heroes. If you read the magazine, you can avoid most pain, maybe even death.

The New Yorker: The idea that there may be a use or lesson in any set of facts is an insult to the intelligence and the sense of humor. The best part of any subject is the fine print, the microdetail. Typographical errors are hilariously funny, hence must be avoided at all costs. The secret of the universe, if it is ever found, will be something quite simple, such as the letter O. Everything is *déjà vu*. It is vulgar to have glands. Erudition can be used only as a "throwaway." In name-dropping, only very obscure names can be dropped. Masses of detail that distract from any possible point improve any story. The best jokes are introversions.

Esquire: Things are not exactly as they seem. The

practical joke is practicable, and qualifies one for the CIA. The *Esquire* office is "where it's happening." The editors, though conscienceless, are awfully smart. The Establishment is more than a little ridiculous. A flat opinion is the only sound one. The lords of the earth are Negro musicians. The old days had their good points.

Ladies' Home Journal: Premarital sex is debatable. Women expect more leadership from their husbands than they get. A woman may marry a man she doesn't love. Women are more reliable than men. Old-fashioned ways should not be lightly discarded. The Bible is not obsolete. Anticipate trouble. Hold the baby while feeding it. Halitosis is not obsolete. Tact is a virtue. Food is very important. (This is by far the most sensible magazine observed here.)

Playboy: Premarital sex is obligatory. Men lead women. Women invariably love men. Anticipate pleasure. Ghastly nightmares are very chic. The big problem is to get a girl's bosom and bottom in the same picture. (It can be done.)

❦ 6 ❦

The Tools of
Ignorance

Anyone who has looked at children's books, usually aimed at teenagers, must have noticed that they are not very different from adult books. Only occasionally is there the telltale condescension, as in "incendiary (fire) bombs." But then one grows more and more aware of a distinct peculiarity in children's books. Even, or especially, on controversial subjects, the text reads like revealed truth or Holy Writ. It is the pot at the end of the search for knowledge. There is no room for doubt. Educators have evidently long since decided that children will not bother to memorize anything that may, just possibly, not be entirely true.

As for adult books, Winston Churchill, on events on which he was the primary source, writes with some caution, nor was he noted for modesty. And even so his works are not without serious error.

Absolute certainty is a mark of ignorance that should

never be overlooked. For example, there is a small juvenile book that presumes to condense the careers of eighteen modern dictators, a task beyond the competence of anybody now alive. In a single paragraph we are told that "a demented Dutch youth set fire to the German Reichstag" and that the Nazi cry was "*Sig heil!*" Whether the Nazis, the Communists, or van der Lubbe set that fire is still in controversy, and the cry was "*Sieg heil!*" for victory.

Absolute certainty is betrayed in another quarter, viz., in government. The intent of government is exactly the same as that of the writers of children's books. It wants us to think it knows what it is doing, especially when it doesn't know what it is doing.

The way to do this is to pervert the substance of the reality into clichés, and then to discuss the reality only in terms of the clichés, or jargon.

Currently we have: replicated, conceptualize, quantified, interfaced, target groups, parameters (grossly misused), maximize, overage (meaning surplus), contextual dynamics, in-service programs, incremental expertise, defoliation, escalation, rectification.

People who use this jargon are esteemed as really knowing what they are talking about. But the one thing we can be sure of is that they don't know what they are talking about. All such expressions are the tools of ignorance. (This last is a cliché commonly applied to the catcher's gear in baseball.)

For example, if the government announces, "We are going to hit the enemy harder," it is saying something real. It sounds more technical and important to say, "We are going to escalate." This may mean merely that more officers in the Pentagon will be put on the job, more money will be allocated, all records will be printed in larger type, or the Secretary of Defense will get a pay raise. The word escalate, in fact, comes from the coined trademark word "escalator," meaning only a moving stairway, which moves both down and up. It could correctly be used to describe orderly evacuation of a war zone.

From government and academe, a language of pretentious ignorance is creeping into general use, as follows:

ALGORITHM. An incorrect variant of algorism, a synonym for arithmetic, using the zero.

ANTENNAE. Tentative communication.

CHRONOLOGICAL PHASING. Escalation in correct sense.

CLASSIFIED. Half-secret.

COEFFICIENT OF COMPATIBILITY. Degree of agreement.

CONSTRUCT. Construction.

COUNTERFORCE. Response.

DEFOLIATION. Atom-bombing trees.

DEMOGRAPHIC RELAXATION. Decline in population.

DICHOTOMY. Division.

DISCRETE CATEGORIES. Self-contained groups.

FAIL-SAFE. Brakes, on second thought.

FIRST-STRIKE CAPABILITY. Pearl Harbor.

GRAY OPERATION. Between official and unofficial.

INFRA-PARTICULAR. ?

MACROSCOPIC ERROR. Big one.

MACRO-STRUCTURE. Ditto.

MEANINGFUL DIALOGUE. Both sides talking.

MENSURABLE. Measurable (special application to music).

MINIMUM DETERRENCE. Cheapest counterforce.

NEXUS. Knot.

NORMATIVE. Normal (special application to minerals).

OPTIMUM. Sounds better than maximum.

PUBLIC SECTOR. Polite word for government.

SCENARIO. Projected schedule or fantasy.

SIMULATION TECHNIQUES. As if.

TELEONOMIC. Not in the dictionary, but probably whole name.

THINK TANK. Thinking underlings.

Jargon (another joke word, meaning originally "twittering," and probably from the same source as "gargoyle") should be a very clear signal that the great men and small men using it are trying to hide under rocks. Why don't they use the ordinary, clear equivalents? The reason is that we would all understand them. Once the cliché has been established, conveying not a meaning but a signal, the citizenry accepts it without alarm, no matter how terrible may be its real content. "Demographic relaxation" might thus be a nice synonym for genocide, now a cliché word which will probably soon be applied to duck-shooting. (The people who use this language do not appear to own dictionaries.) The ridiculous word "escalation" may very well usher in World War III.

The process ought to be familiar. Anyone who wants to teach or pontificate or rule has to make a list of words which replace the realities. For Hitler, "Non-Aryan" was the replacement for "Jew," or "Slav," or anybody he didn't like. The word had the mystical power to make these people disappear from German consideration. The same function is served in the American South by "nigger" and in the North by "whitey" or "honkie." In each case the cliché overpowers the observable and varying reality. The Negro who uses the derogation of the white is as corrupted as the Southerner who uses the derogation of the black, or as the Nazi by his insult to the "Non-Aryans." In every case, the cliché is hung around their necks. And in every case it is happy instinct to accept the cliché. The cliché makes them all happy, just as "first-strike capability" makes generals happy. The cliché is better than Santa Claus.

When people are uncomfortable or confused with the reality, enter the cliché. Ignorance is, not unnaturally, the general condition of any government of an area larger than a small village. Governments are therefore in the business of amassing clichés, mostly called laws or statutes, which are substituted for realities.

As was noted earlier, clichés can usher in revolution.

Revolt *against* clichés can also usher in revolution. The current peculiar and obstreperous behavior of young people may be, at bottom and probably in part unconsciously, a claustrophobic convulsion against a world of stultifying clichés.

Still, the revolt is unreasonable. In a large society, information must be issued in the schools in such a way that it can be used in all parts of the society. Furthermore, examinations must be given to see which students have "received" the information. An examination on the reality of anything is very difficult to compose, and the answers would be impossible to grade. An examination on received clichés is easy to compose, and the answers are either right or wrong. For example, a student who knew the subject in depth would fail the course. The required answer for "Who set the Reichstag fire?" is van der Lubbe, demented Dutch youth. A thousand words of well-informed speculation is wrong. Having passed that course, the student goes on to another set of clichés. If his interest and thinking powers are utterly numbed, one can sympathize.

Modern pedagogy is dehumanized and eviscerated by its belief that any subject must be turned into a neat, self-contained system. The idea that one might get interested in history via Genghis Khan, the Crusades, Richard Coeur de Lion, Don John, Charles V, and so on, is a horror and a nightmare to the modern pedagogue. But such a student will never lose his interest in history.

The current style of systematizing unsystematizable knowledge blankets the schools. A trivial but delightfully revealing example of it surfaced when a scholar type set out to explain the "British" or pun-anagram kind of crossword puzzle. There are about twenty kinds of clues in these puzzles, and the best way to explain them is to give examples. The interest lies in the fact that the puzzler never knows which kind he is working on. However, our pseudo-scholar systematized the matter into "seven basic kinds of clues. (1) Anagrams. (2) Multiple meanings. (3) Reversals. (4) Charades. (5) Container and contents. (6) Puns. (7) Hidden." The only virtue of this list is that an examination can easily be given the student on whether he has mastered the list. The fact that he now has no desire to play the game is beside the pedagogue's point.

This same system is used in nearly every textbook, for example, the venerable standard Preston James's *An Outline of Geography.* Here in eight instead of seven categories we are given the cliché, or fossilized, system of areas of the earth: (1) Dry. (2) Tropical

Forest. (3) Mediterranean Scrub Forest. (4) Mid-Latitude Mixed Forest. (5) Grasslands. (6) Boreal Forest. (7) Polar. (8) Mountain. An argument can be presented that the list does not include forest steppe, tundra, swamp, and the peculiar Southeastern United States with the needleleaf evergreen on a red-yellow podzolic soil. The list, in short, follows the pattern of freezing the "right" answers into a cliché, and excluding all sorts of unamenable reality.

When James gets down to particulars, he notes that "The dry lands . . . are deficient in moisture. . . . Rains come only at infrequent and irregular intervals. . . . Temperatures in the dry lands vary considerably according to the latitude." A bright student, on reading this, might throw the book out the window or abandon the subject. But this planet, that is, geography, may well be the most interesting subject in the universe. And the rest of James's book is interesting, as most geographies are.

The same teaching system has planted its skeletal grip even on such a serious, adult activity as war. Napoleon once had some brilliant and workable ideas on the subject, applied in action. An intellectual, Clausewitz, closely studied all that was known about Napoleon's performances and abstracted some cliché theories on the "perfect" conduct of war, viz., concentration, security, mobility. These clichés have since been taught in all military academies, and revered by all professional officers, without noticeably raising the incidence of Napoleons. The conclusion might be that the successful officer, with or without Clausewitz, must finally depend on his own personal sense of reality, his brains, character, and will.

Nobody has had any brilliant ideas about war lately, and so Herman Kahn, an intellectual, has systematized this lack of ideas in a book, *On Escalation*, which reflects the current wars and theorizes on atomic war. It has been violently criticized as antihuman, as if even mentioning atomic war were bad manners, as would have been the mention of legs to a Victorian lady. It should instead be criticized for giving cliché words to the factors of war for government and the military. As of presidents and officers, it can be characterized as a perfect exercise in castration.

On such a fatal subject, the technique is interestingly true to the model. The obvious is stated in a form of words. For example, one side wins if the other does not fight. (Why, yes, how true.) A war can be increased in area, in intensity, or by taking on more enemies. (How true.) Some wars (Vietnam), like labor strikes, are not intended to destroy the enemy but to pressure for compromise. Other wars (Israel-Arabs) are like boys' auto games of "chicken." The former is labeled "agreed battle." A nation's possibilities of action are listed as contractual, coercive, agonistic (actually meaning "competitive," but here used as decent competition), stylistic (meaning "traditional"), and familial (meaning "friendly"). This list follows the form of those cited above, raising fossil clichés over the tombs of the realities, and making it nearly impossible to think about reality.

With every precious word of this, we get farther and farther from what is actually going to happen. We almost forget that people, not just heads-of-state but whole masses of people, are in deadly earnest and can be roused to mass murderous rages. A score of examples have been presented already in this century, and the century is far from finished. Agonistic, stylistic, familial, forget it.

The historical fact is that the American people, like any indifferent democratic people, are very slow to rage, as in World Wars I and II. They have no particular desire to lower the boom on anybody. But Kahn asserts that Americans tend to take strong moral stands (this reflects a lunatic belief that this is still a Puritan society), indulge in suicidal threats, and take excessive risks.

History makes absolute nonsense of all this. The reactions to Pearl Harbor, South Korea, or South Vietnam can hardly be described as frivolous moral stands, accompanied by wild threats or foolish risks. In every case the enemy did not want to compromise. The enemy, in Kahn's own word, was coercive. Perhaps he should invent a new word for one's moral stand when one is "coerced." A modest suggestion in that case is the old word "rage." Not even the most kindly liberals would substitute the fashionable word "permissive." Even they would sympathize with the desire of the whole American people to survive as a society. The way things are going, the whole free world should pray for the continued existence of the United States.

The plan of Kahn's book is the metaphor of a ladder leading into World War III. The word for climbing a scaling ladder is in fact "escalade." This remarkable ladder should be defined as going down into the pit, rather than up.

But so powerful is a cliché that Kahn prints his ladder as going up, not down. For his title is *On Escalation.*

The ladder has forty-four "rungs" or academically ver-
balized stages, like the seven kinds of crossword puzzle
clues or the eight kinds of land area, paralyzed into fossil
clichés. Rung No. 1 is, unominously, "Ostensible Crisis."
It takes twenty-one rungs to reach "Local Nuclear War
—Exemplary." This ushers in a phase defined as "Bi-
zarre Crisis," meaning either "odd" or, in its original
Basque derivation, "bearded" or "manly." The final
rung, No. 44, is "Spasm or Insensate War," and that's
the top of the ladder or the bottom of the pit. Except
for unspecified "Aftermath," the most interesting stage
of all.

Of course Mr. Kahn's vision of the future is defective.
He has overlooked the North Vietnamese "rung" of infiltrating and seizing the central cities in early 1968.
Another "rung," the kidnapping of key executives,
failed in Vietnam and did not make Kahn's ladder. And
so on. For one must never forget that wars will sometimes be fought by people who have not read the
book.

Nevertheless, Kahn's attempt to "program" or "scenario" World War III is very far from wicked; the intent in fact is noble. The graduations of the oncoming
holocaust, as he graphs them, are not exactly anything
that should be depended upon. Still, he brings out the
sensible point that there would be very little advantage in atom-bombing the great cities until the very
late stages—a point I made in print as long ago as 1959.
Much of that forgotten essay is echoed here, quite (I
would think) unconsciously, for the basic factors are
obvious to anyone who will think about the "scenario"
objectively and unhysterically.

A real danger is that Herman Kahn has pre-fossilized

World War III into a set of cliché fantasies and that when the "ostensible crisis" comes, the American chiefs will be studying the doctrinaire table, while the enemy is furiously concentrating on the real situation. In this case, the enemy has a great advantage.

It may be excessive to say that the man who has not read the book has the advantage. It would be better to say that the man who does not believe the book has the advantage.

An inherent flaw in all such thinking as Kahn's is apparent. A great many, if not most, human affairs are decided by kind, not degree; that is, by quality, not quantity. Kahn's methods try to convert qualities into the more manageable quantities. They thus pretend to have abolished the qualities. In merchandising, in art, in politics, in war, quality has overcome quantity too often to submit to any such treatment. Even when quantity wins, it is beyond its power to destroy quality. Quantities rise and fall; qualities remain.

An indication that Kahn may actually have turned contemporary warfare into clichés is given by the Vietnam War. Anyone who has not read his book must see that war as a meaningless ballet or a Lewis Carroll charade. But the war becomes perfectly intelligible, if not sensible, after a reading of the book.

For example, America's refraining from the use of the atom bomb would be admirable, if nobody knew that we had one, and were refraining from its use. But since everybody knows we have it, our not using it is a blow to South Vietnamese morale, and a refreshment to North Vietnamese morale. America does not even hint that it might just possibly use the bomb, or invade the

north. Such forbearance is admirable until some time
after thirty-five thousand young Americans have died
for this bluffless poker game.

The essential curse on our presence in Vietnam may
be that we are again cleaning up a French mess, a
chore that has occupied us over the past fifty years.
During that time France has been a latent or overt
disaster, or perhaps one should make it 150 years,
since the cliché that has ruined France is Napoleon.
Similarly, the American South has been ruined by the
cliché R. E. Lee. France and the South have evidently
not yet paid in full for their clichés.

Before we finish with Kahn, still another, more crip-
pling, fallacy must be noted. The most gifted novelists
and playwrights know that to reproduce anything re-
sembling "real life" is far beyond them, and do not
attempt it. For in real life thousands of the factors are
unknown. Just as the hero is solving his personal tragedy, a total stranger is taking a tenth drink in a bar
and will, an hour later, swerve his car so as to force
a woman driver to skid into an accident in which the
hero will be killed, disabled, or blinded. Or large hidden economic or technological changes on the other
side of the planet end by putting the hero out of business. Or an obscure episode in his wife's childhood may
have left her with a latent character flaw that will ruin
his life. In international affairs, the unknown factors
come in the billions.

Of course Kahn realizes this. In describing his pro-
jections or "scenarios" he modestly uses the word "plausible." Plausible certainly; but a plausible science or art
is not much good. Plausible to whom? To a high-school

boy? To the chiefs of staff? To the Kremlin? The un-
friendly will substitute "specious."

But I must compliment Kahn on his vocabulary for
the discussion of World War III. It may improve the
conversation. But it will not improve World War III.

✎ 7 ✎

The Alienation Cliché

Decent, kindly, intelligent young people have told me that America is abominable. They are the supine victims of the anti-cliché cliché. They know no history, no geography, no morality. And of course America is abominable, for America is populated by people. What they think the other political areas of the planet are populated by, I do not profess to know.

We might therefore inquire into this anti-cliché cliché.

The situation is that nearly half the American population must be educated simultaneously, and this education is a fixed prerequisite to well-paid employment. The law of supply and demand immediately goes into effect. Good, not to speak of great, teachers have always been in short supply, and may properly prefer not to address their remarks to this rabble. Knowledge is aristocratic; the aristocrat may choose not to

share his knowledge with hoodlums who would prefer
to burn down his college, including his lifetime of research. The demand is there; the supply is not. The demand will increase inevitably; the supply will decrease,
fatally.

In this situation the education must consist of mass-
produced and mass-distributed clichés. Faced with
mobs who want degrees rather than educations, the
best-motivated system can dispense nothing else. Most
degrees of bachelor, master, and doctor, in this world
of cliché personnel screening, are empty clichés prov-
ing the recipient's ability to parrot, and little more.
Ambitious children and parents nevertheless want those
credentials, and will accept the clichés.

But the young are quite capable of recognizing this
nonsense for what it is. Their revolt, as has been indicated, is instinctive and claustrophobic, an explosion
against they know not what. They can't think for themselves, and nobody has told them, that they are not
satisfied with clichés. Another element in the revolt is
suicidal and infantile narcissism, but this is a trait not
invented by the current generation of youth, and so
one that can be dismissed from local consideration.

The substitute for the cliché is the whole complex
uncertain truth as best one can know it, complete with
misgivings. It is not the anti-cliché cliché. But in the
universities we are dealing with young professors who
desperately want reputations and followings among the
youth. They are thus in the business of devising anti-
cliché clichés.

A suitable example is Leslie Fiedler in *Love and
Death in the American Novel*. Fiedler often refers to
"our country," meaning, one gathers in context, Amer-

ica, or the United States of America. He was in fact born in America, in Newark, New Jersey. Though the surname may be unfamiliar, library files show that there have been a great crowd of distinguished, or at least verbal, Fiedlers, not the least verbal being Leslie.

The cliché against which he revolts is, one must suppose, that "our country" is a reasonably decent or even magnificent society. Now here comes Fiedler.

First, the same forces produced the Declaration of Independence and the Marquis de Sade. Both made the convict the judge, the pervert the natural man, and death better than life. (Pray believe me, this is what the man says. The book is available to all.)

Second, all American literature is "a Gothic fiction of darkness."

Third, America is "a world without a significant history or a substantial past." This expression reveals that the wildest sort of raving is permissible today. But let us take it seriously. It means either that the Ghibellines, the Fronde, the Inquisition, and the Wars of the Roses are not part of the white American past, or that these events were somehow nobler, classier, more substantial and significant than anything that has happened in America, such as the frontier, the Revolution, the Civil War, and so on. No significant history, no substantial past, no czars, no pogroms, no guillotines, no dynasties, alas.

Fourth, the quality of the American is "embarrassment with love, obsession with violence." This calls for serious discussion. The old American is not embarrassed by love but it may perhaps be generalized that he would prefer to avoid it; love is a weakening. The American is obsessed by will, not by violence. But in many times and places he would not have survived if he had not been at home with violence. So much is true. The American's opinions of love and violence are not inscrutable; they are primarily functional in terms of practical experience. Fiedler comes to them like a man from the moon. A schoolgirl is as qualified to discuss Clausewitz on war as Fiedler to describe the American.

Throughout, Fiedler's angle of vision is that there was something subtly and inherently wicked about the white man's "discovery" and settling of America. (How wicked were the Angles and Saxons in England?) Faced with the inexplicable, my intuition is that the wickedness lies in the fact that the conquistadors and Pilgrims were not named Fiedler, Fiedler, Fiedler, that the contemporary Fiedlers were then festering in some shameful slum, and that he cannot forgive America, Therefore, he conducts a tantrum on the pillows, substituting mere wildness for thought, knowing that the children will believe anything that destroys the cliché. That Fiedler is exactly that trivial is my honest belief.

There are other delicacies in this fruitcake of the anti-cliché cliché. For example, *Huckleberry Finn* is a "desperate attempt to convince us of the innocence of violence, the good clean fun of horror." Accepting the fact that this is a book for children, Fiedler theorizes that the American novel is, in general, childish. He solves the difficulty of equating horror and childishness by saying that "a child's world is full of terrors." And thus the package is wrapped up. Well, I was a child once, and my world was not "full of terrors," and I knew other children, and their worlds were not "full of terrors." There are at the moment nearly two billion children in the world, and this man presumes to describe their "world" in a universal generalization to make a point about the American novel.

But Fiedler's insolence now comes to *Moby Dick*, which is, among other things, an authoritative description of the sailing technique of the time. As realism, it seems to Fiedler "a scandalous botch." He is wrong, but even if he were right, his language is intemperate. He takes the archetype of the American hero to be Rip van Winkle, because Rip ran away from his wife. His dismissal of Edgar Allan Poe is entirely based on an attempt at hackwork, *The Narrative of Arthur Gordon Pym*.

Not knowing what he is talking about is no embarrassment to Fiedler. It is in fact his ideal métier, the particular air in which he sky-dives with the parachute of his glib, resourceful verbalization.

It must be conceded that Fiedler brings to the intellectual process all the lofty objectivity and love of truth and justice of a juvenile mugger in an alley. A thing he might have said about American writers is that they often confuse the act of writing with the acquisition of power. They want to intimidate people as much as do policemen, judges, doctors, dentists, sergeants, generals, teachers, preachers, and political commentators. The vice is especially prevalent right now, and of course Fiedler shares it in an advanced stage. (Incidentally, he tells one joke I like: Cristoforo Colombo means Christ-bearing dove. Very good.)

The vestigial benefit in reading Fiedler is that you will have something surprising to say: a cliché that few adults will have heard, though the children all know it.

True, it will be nonsense but it will be chic, for it will blackguard "our country" for all the wrong reasons. Misrepresenting America is the fashionable cliché in the present period. White adult males are the chief substance of America, and they are under attack simultaneously by Negroes, children, women, and homosexuals, with the general support of the intellectuals (excluding myself).

The more recent waves of new Americans certainly have no obligation whatever to admire the existing American culture as they find it; their disdain and rejections are exemplary and creative. It is true that European critics of European cultures typically have some fifty generations of hereditary familiarity behind them. America can aspire to no more than five or ten generations as a rule. Its major criticism, however, comes from Americans of two or three generations. Their status as Americans is utterly beyond cavil. My only complaint is that when they look at me they do not know what they see.

❧ 8 ❧

The Clique Cliché

This is the most amusing and neglected of all subjects. The Plato set in Athens, the knights of the Round Table, the douzepers of Charlemagne, the Inquisition priesthood, the Vatican, all sets of courtiers, the Quakers, the Whigs in England, the Bloomsbury set in London, the Algonquin set in New York, The New Yorker set today, all of which have inevitably become clichés, are the historic examples of the cliché clique.

Luckily we have at hand a contemporary clique, unknown to most people, which has some of the essential traits of the older cliché groups, and this was arbitrarily forced on my attention by a direction to Norman Podhoretz's *Making It*. This young man has a gorgeous intellectual narcissism, a quality that English teachers inexplicably dote on and which brought his teachers, he says, into dotage. The adult apotheosis of verbal youth (which, to console Podhoretz, I will admit I also

received) is likely to launch a conceited youth into the
great world. The late Whittaker Chambers had this
same gift of intellectual narcissism, and hypnotized able
Columbia teachers.

I was ordered to read Podhoretz on the assumption
that he would revolt me. He did not, at all. True, he
writes a sinking sentence, which is as liquid as a piece
of string, loosely in the manner of Matthew Arnold as
strained through Lionel Trilling of Columbia. Still, it is
a transparent, legible, and reasonable style, carrying
surprisingly small content but sufficient interest. The
sentences do not have well-defined subjects and predicates. This fact reveals that when he begins a sentence
he has not completed a thought; he has only contem-
plated it: not quite enough. Indeed, he admits that he
considers writing as an exercise in itself, not, as it is,
as a mere side-effect of correct thinking and feeling. In
his clique delusion, he excludes himself and his coterie
from the great men of the culture.

Who am I to criticize? Well, the language in which
the foregoing was stated (visible to the reader) is
legible and reasonable, not entirely transparent, heavy
on subjects and predicates, and reflects unitary completed thoughts, any one of which could be supported
by several thousand more words. The preceding sentence, for example, has a heavy subject and a heavy
predicate. That's a sentence. In contrast, Podhoretz is
never sure what he is talking about: a winning trait.

Podhoretz describes his clique as "the family," meaning the Jewish writers for *Commentary* and also *Partisan Review*, but the actual writers are mostly Gentile,
in the issue I examined. "Family" will be used herein-
after to designate Podhoretz's clique.

Podhoretz first explains that he and his friends are generally second- or third-generation Russian Jews, that is, lower class by birth, but that he is now upper middle class on merit. (Why not upper class, if he has the option?) Even the immigrants just off the boat have far greater tact and delicacy than the upper-class natives. The New York intellectual world is almost exclusively composed of Russian Jews. The people described are attractive Americans. The whole book is about ambition, which is always called ambitiousness.

But to define and ennoble their clique, these excellent people have thought their way into cliché lunacy. "America did not belong to them." (Why not?) "Jewishness . . . a valuable asset in that it rendered them doubly alienated from American society." (This is good?) The family has more serious intelligence than the rest of America. (Huh?) "The feeling that this was not my country; I was not really part of it . . . I was as ghettoized as my ancestors." (Pure attitudinizing.) The family's black beasts are *kitsch* (honest German word for "trash" or "popular art," but meaning almost anything here, probably *South Pacific*, not comic strips. Not derived from Algonquinian *kitchi manito*), middlebrows, commercialism, mass culture, academicism, populism, liberalism, Stalinism. "Integrity and standards were only possible among" the family. German Jews can't write English.

The idea seems to be that to like anything about America is to become a counterfeit white Anglo-Saxon Protestant (WASP). But in liking the family he is liking part of America, though not quite as all-conquering a part as the family imagines. In making the clique and America antitheses, the family cannot see any

American reality as it is. For example, we read "The great majority of American literary people in the thirties were Stalinists."

I was around then, and the sentence would be greatly improved by the addition of "not." Indeed, I went to the same high school and college as Podhoretz, and early associated with the very people who have become his elder Jewish heroes; some I liked or "loved" (a word he uses carelessly—perhaps as a demonstration of Jewish tact and delicacy), some, not.

As opposed to the mass of America, the family must be expressing an admirable loyalty to their Yiddish-speaking parents. But the parents will soon be dead. The only permanent ideal that can remain is the memory of Pinsk in the year 1900, as if that had been a golden Camelot. Pinsk, it must be noted, a thousand years old, was burned by the Poles, the Russians, and the Swedes, and frequently pogromized. Their dream can thus be seen to be a nightmare, not very nutritious.

Surely such resourceful sophists can find *something* about America more nourishing, which would also furnish the required clique cement. If the family does not like German-American Jews, how about Sephardic Jews who, fleeing an earlier Inquisition, reached New York in the early seventeenth century, after a perilous odyssey? If the prompting is impertinent, forgive me.

A few more clichés of this clique can be offered. Mankind needs heroes but usually finds hideous impostors. Fame is better than money or power (but not really). The title of Writer confers a very lofty rank. The idea that maturity was better than youth began to dissolve in the late 1950s. Jewishness became chic in the 1960s. The belief that no Communist could be decent (*vide* Koestler and Orwell) was permanently repealed by Khrushchev's secret anti-Stalin speech, evidently on the grounds that the speech was an act of exemplary decency. (Eh?) The family can and does attack its own membership. The relationships, or psychic genealogy, within the family, as in any clique, are far too complex and trivial for transcription.

The voice of the clique—perhaps we can call it the Pinsk clique—does not directly reach all Americans. Podhoretz thinks that his magazine, *Commentary*, reaches one hundred thousand circulation, about that of *Time* in the early 1930s. But I think it is entitled to some credit for promulgating ideas that forward the demoralization of America. As of the magazines described earlier, it certainly has some influence on the editors of *The New Yorker, Esquire, Playboy*, is familiar to Time Inc., and probably to all of the others.

The *Commentary* strategy might be laughingly defined as selling America short in the hope of buying it back cheap. To the family it is absolutely inconceivable that there can be a single intelligent patriot. For all cliques live in this singular darkness, the black night of shutting one's eyes to other values.

Apparently we are obliged to synopsize an issue of *Commentary*.

The first discovery one makes in this magazine (and also in *Partisan Review*) is that just as one thinks an essay is ending, one finds that it is only starting. The doubtful conclusions of the first part become the major premises of the syllogisms of the second part, and one must go on reading. This trope is called "sorites," which describes a corrupt sophistry of medieval Catholic theology, here oddly embraced by Jews. Perhaps we will need more than one simple sentence to give the point of the *Commentary* pieces.

The June 1968 issue opens with the major premise, acceptable enough, that central authority is being defied everywhere today. The minor premise is that this defiance is merely a speeded-up version of the normal democratic process. Thus, the conclusion is that a truly progressive society must welcome disorder and violence. (A surprising corollary: not everybody is entitled to an education.)

On these assumptions, the "populism" of Senator Eugene McCarthy is that of an imbecile professor who knows nothing of the cities. The weakness of populism is that it is interested in emotional issues, such as the draft and black power, and not in what the writer is interested in. (The latter's interests: A-bomb. Pollution. Automation. Decentralization. Research. Education. Foreign Aid. Cities. How to weaken the nation-state.)

Here, in a wildly dogmatic form, we see again the signs of the juvenile book, the tools of ignorance, total omniscience, with no room for questioning, only the need to pass the examination. If the author is so superior to McCarthy, why not nominate him for President?

Next comes a fine piece on Israel, twenty pages.

Next, a piece saying that white-black hostility is cresting, though cooperation between militant blacks and police cooled the first 1968 riots in the cities. But the American city, unlike the European city, has played no part in history, and presumably will not start now.

(Footnote: Boston and Philadelphia started the American Revolution. New York produced Hamilton, Jay, Livingston, Morris; Philadelphia, at least Franklin. New

Orleans invented creole culture. St. Louis supplied the frontier west. San Francisco was the gold rush. Boston, Mass., and Charleston, S.C., invented the Civil War. Chicago was a complete phase of the American culture and boast. Pittsburgh is steel; Detroit, the automobile; New York, the capital of the world. What a marvelous climate where one is allowed to publish the statement that the American city is a cipher.)

In these cities live 75 per cent of American Negroes, the "vast majority" of adults born in the South. ("Statistics" questionable.) The current plan, inferentially bad, is to make the Negro fit for the city, not the city fit for the Negro. (Sounds good to me.) Southern states are calculatedly dumping unrehabilitatable Negroes on the North, and black activists in the North are increasing. (True. But good?) Hence, the Army is expected to conduct summer maneuvers in the Northern ghettoes. (Says who?) Negroes demand that American foreign policy be subordinated to the problem of the cities, traditionally unimportant.

The authors speak as Negro popes, without credentials. Their syllogism is a bedlam, unless one understands that any new way of saying that America stinks is a brilliant insight. Again we sense these people's distaste for the newness of America. But America is not quite that new. No mortal man can call 350 years a minute. It is these people who are new, and they are not glad they made the trip. The shadow of golden Pinsk still shimmers over all, blotting out the American achievement, which can be objectively rated as a little more remarkable than even the Israeli achievement, noted above. (Disproving this would make a fine piece for *Commentary*.)

Through these pieces runs, besides the obvious snobbery, a soothsayer strain of divination, of magical insight as foretelling the future.

And so the next piece says that nobody has ever been able to predict the future, and cancels them out. The usual seers, and we have them in numbers today, foresee that certain present curves will be projected into the future in artistic graphlines. World population in A.D. 2000 will be five billion, or maybe eight billion. (Highly unlikely.) This author gives the example of rolling dice, where a long series of rolls gives no indication whatever of the next roll. The problem of prediction is still worse. The equation at the present moment is creating new factors that will considerably change the equation, but these billions of factors are unknown, and the new equation is utterly unpredictable. The one thing one knows about a present situation is that when it matures it will be a little, or greatly, different. Hitler's career is a sufficient example: the situation matured a little. The writer flatly contradicts Liebnitz: "the present is *not* big with the future." From any present, a million varying futures can be extrapolated. The writer tells *Commentary* something it evidently does not know: a very great deal of the present will remain, usually more than will be lost. But the magazine does not know even what is present today.

Next comes a swelling hymn to James Baldwin, the Negro writer, who is evidently one of the family, though not from Pinsk. Hardly a review of a book (elsewhere scorned), the piece predicts that whites and blacks, the rich, the Establishment, will decide the Negro's place finally "without understanding." More soothsaying, of the uncheckable kind.

Next comes a piece on TV specials comparing them to protean man with polymorphous versatility, that is, without character.

Next comes an apparently innocent travel feature on Iquitos, Peru (mistakenly calling it the former rubber headquarters), which turns into a sly satire on the evolution of the brave frontiersman into the exploiter. Who but the American pioneer is the target?

Next comes a delightful thesis that all stories of sex are like fish stories: they are essentially lies. Sex is a private pleasure; when it is conveyed publicly it must turn into a lie, intended to inspire envy and emulation, not comprehension. Excellent.

Since Hitler, reconciliation has come to Jews and Christians, both facing God and honoring each other.

The norm of American life is stupefied, cliché banality, expressed in a book by a brilliant product of precisely that life.

Modern prizewinning scientists are no longer gentlemen. Nonspecialization has begun to pay off big.

Finally, a review of a book on European Jewish history.

As can be seen, some good sense asserts itself; the whole issue is a mix, doubtless on some editorial theory. On the literary level, *Commentary* is about the equal of *Playboy*, though of course somewhat less readable.

◄§ 9 §►

The Children's Cliché

How dare one call any generation of children a cliché? Every generation is always the hope and darling of mankind, and can do no unpardonable wrong. If the laws that pamper juveniles assume that they are idiots, an apple tree in blossom is still more charming than an apple tree in fruit after the bugs have worked on it: the promise is always better than the fulfillment. Criticism of the current youth is permissible only to those who enjoyed their own youth, enjoyed rebellion, and have some standards for rebellious youth.

The far-out part of the current youth thing is satire or farce on itself: these people cannot be serious. A boy with long hair and a beard cannot sleep comfortably on his back or his front; in a fight he can be yanked around at will; he is in danger around any machine; he is likely to support a population of lice;

he dirties his shirts faster; he probably smells; by making himself an eyesore, he hides.

This character has a philosophy, if one may dignify it, which does not get the courtesy of an ideological reply. The omission is herewith briefly remedied. Horror is indeed a part of life, but should be suppressed. Illusions are often the best part of life, and might well be preserved; any attendant neurosis is not all that bad. The word love has always been utterly indefinable. Excellence is preferable to incompetence. Some people are superior in any particular function to some other people. Competition, or conflict, is native to the temperate zone, where winter sometimes comes. Being conspicuous, particularly offensively so, has always been the easy way to become extinct. The final test of a society is how much useful energy it generates. The whole society's responsibility does not extend to the individual's "self-expression"; that is the individual's business. This much is surely enough to outrage the childish minority, but it is a reply.

What these youths are essentially saying is that there is only one significant person in the world, much as Marx and Lenin said. But unlike Marx and Lenin, they cannot invent any intelligible description of this significant person, and so they fall back on: just like me. Faced with other significant persons, they resort to the hollow four-letter words (in which only they believe) and the barrages of ordure, this last being their own authentic creation, the indubitable end-product of their pampered affluence, and its redolent memento.

The cliché definition of these youth is "cool." Clearly this does not mean cool in the sense of being poised, calm, courageous, as under fire. The dictionary has another meaning: "presumptuous or impudent; negligent of conventional diffidence or consideration in manner toward others." It seems roughly applicable. Since they cannot define themselves, let it stand.

The children being discussed are a small minority, but they set the style. This must be described for the sake of an incredulous posterity. The leader types have soft, wide-open, vulnerable eyes; the followers, sullen eyes. A faint guilty smirk, as of a bedwetter, is common. The great dusty face-bush and fall of dirty head-hair are signals or clichés. The borderline "squares" with their sideburns cannot imitate the flamboyant shoulders, hands and hips, splay-legged walk, horizontal position, abandon, effrontery, dirtiness, and lust for intimacy.

These children are looking for something. They say it is love. As their life style clearly indicates, what they are looking for is horror, and the place to look for this commodity is in oneself, and anyone can find it. For the relatively innocent young to look for it is an obscene precocity. When I was younger, I remembered and regretted nothing. As I get older, I begin to recall horrible things I have done and suffered, but I hope to dismiss them until I am dead. Children who cherish horror, which they call love, are nearly senile.

In defiance of all known natural law, the pace-setters and image-makers of youth have become the flawed, the rejects, the defectives, the bedwetters, the queers. How such an inversion of nature came about deserves our most searching interest.

One theory is that it is a latter and decadent stage of liberalism by whose rules the criminal is sick, not bad, the stupid are only disadvantaged, the poor are not responsible for themselves, the drug addict is a victim, cowards are heroic peace-lovers, brave men are death-wishers, homosexuals are normal, the normal are latent homosexuals, defects are lovable, excellence is unfair to incompetence, everybody is only human. Virtue thus becomes an embarrassment, and vice takes the name of its alibi. Once judgment is suspended, morality abolished, the virtuous are the helpless victims of the defectives. Naturally the old liberalism, for all its high nobility of intent, has become a cliché, or joke. Down is up, bad is good, left is right, black is white, and the points of the compass are scrambled.

Another theory is that the youth is rebelling against clichés, meaning, most insistently, TV and radio commercials. Certainly the air is full of transparent lies, often set to winning music. The tunes make the words insulting nonsense. Charming voices beguile one with a melody to which the words are "Before you sign on the dotted line, know what your loan will CAW-W-W-ST." The nonsense is everywhere. When an institution has passed far beyond caring, it advertises, "Who cares? A & P cares." These bald and naïve attempts at brainwashing, repeated on every side, may well build a slowly accumulating rage and contempt in the young. The elements of atrocious satire are the everyday stuff of the society.

Another theory is that the jobs in a huge, enormously complex industrial and bureaucratic system are seen as offering insufficient scope for the expression of the youths' unfocused talents.

Another theory is that the young simply do not want to go to work, that is, to deal with problems created by situations presented by somebody else. There is

some merit in this theory. Some petted city dogs are so
corrupted that they freeze in the presence of a larger
dog; they do not even know enough to run away; they
are not fit to survive. The minority of defective youth
shares this fatal decadence. Their "love" really means
"I can't defend myself, please," as they collapse on the
floor in their favorite horizontal position. They deserve
the name "horizontal generation," one that will be
trampled by the crowds of new men and women who
want the jobs these *fainéants* have abdicated. The society has a wall-to-wall carpeting of hairy dropouts,
which will delight the young, talented Negroes who
want the jobs. Some sons of corporation vice-presidents
think their fathers' jobs are humiliating clichés, and
care only about who they are. They raise that wonderful cry to the sky, "Why was I born?" The black boy
knows exactly who he is, and he wants the job.

Another theory is that the adults have no beliefs held
strongly enough to be worth enforcing on the young.
This one is getting closer to the matter. Babies are delightful; small children are charming; but a permis-
sively reared child becomes an abomination to everybody by the ages of thirteen to fifteen. The important
thing the parents do not believe in at about that stage
is the child himself. One child stabbed a father who
tried to tell him who was supporting him. It was far
too late. The father was not an ancient and sacred
social figure; he was merely the car, the TV set, the
bed, the meals, the allowance. The youth had all this
without effort, gratitude, love, or obligation. He might
have gathered that he was an object of love, or at least
of attention, if the father had slugged him. But the

parents do not love their children enough to enforce their dim beliefs.

The new children mature, copulate, and have babies. Are they, too, permissive? Ah, no, they exhibit a growing tendency to beat their babies to death. The inner rage of this "father" is naturally directed against what is nearest and most vulnerable, that is, the baby. His "thing" is to kill the baby. After all, it is his baby. In contrast to his kindly, permissive parents, he deeply believes in something. Guess what. Himself, and nothing else.

Each of these theories contributes something to understanding the defective minority of youth.

But still another theory is preferred by those who have read V. C. Wynne-Edwards' *Animal Dispersion in Relation to Social Behavior*. The theory is that the whole animal kingdom has systems of communication that signal when populations have passed the optimum and command a cutback in reproduction. The creatures feel overcrowded. The methods of population control include neuroticism of males and females, deterioration of females' ova, exclusion of inferior males from breeding, sterile eggs or quick-dying young, cannibalism of the young, desertion, prolonged adolescence, reduced breeding, reduced litters, mutual harassment, abortions or uterine resorptions, and homosexuality. Modern human society has experimented with about eight of these population controls.

Some people object to being compared to other animals—a snobbery that ill becomes this species. For the self-destructive life style of the image-making youthful minority does come close enough to Wynne-

Edwards' pattern for the lower species when over-crowded. It is exactly the minority who ought not to breed who are setting the style. Being normal, that is, enjoying the opposite sex and loving babies, is dismissed with contempt as "square." The self-destructive youth have rejected everything desirable: comfort, cleanliness, manners, good sense, consideration, self-respect, a goal in life, the future, the past. They are perfectly programed to become extinct.

This is of course not the youthful minority's picture of themselves. They believe they are conducting a revolution. A revolution is against something, certainly, but it is also for something. The children's revolution has gotten only as far as the first half, if that far. Sympathetic youth-watchers have tried to find some coherent program, anything, that the youth believe in. So far, in vain.

But what they are against is almost equally insubstantial. Their extreme rantings about America or the Establishment or the present organization of society have no real content. They might well protest against the utilities, the insurance companies, Detroit, highways, pollution, advertising, but these are either inaccessible to them, or outside their narrow areas of interest. And so, like the youth who kills his baby, they revolt blindly against what is nearest: parents, teachers, colleges, communities, all of which are usually quite innocent and unprepared. The brilliant victories of these youth are won only over those who, foolishly, love them.

And so at this point it is customary to avow that the revolutionary minority of youth is the finest, wisest, most dedicated generation in all the years of man and that, even if they may not be quite that, they are the overwhelming wave of the world. This avowal will be conspicuously omitted here.

How can one describe a generation of the immature as "the finest" anything? Nevertheless, a few valid predictions can be made for the far-out minority of this generation. First, an unusual number of suicides may be noted among them, and this rate will certainly increase in the next ten years. Second, and more harmlessly, marijuana smokers tend to get fat. Third, since prolonged exposure to very high-decibel music injures the ears, they will be nearly deaf. Fourth, since the new pastime of staring into bright lights ruins the eyes, they will be nearly blind. Fifth, numbers of LSD users will become mentally incompetent, deranged, and useless, overloading the asylums.

Suicidal, deaf, blind, crazy, and overweight: "the finest generation"! The finest of its kind since Sodom and Gomorrah. The whole society, which they find so revolting, had better prepare to take care of them in their chronological prime, for they will be already senile. Still, a genius or two may emerge; this is not impossible. But at what a cost!

The remainder of the youth may deserve the very highest marks in due time. The black youth are certainly their "finest generation," but the next ought to be still finer.

The youthful indictment of the society is, most cogently, that it has become a set of clichés. But the youth now number over a billion. That fact alone makes them the cliché, mass-produced and all imprecisely more or less alike. In twenty countries they even act alike. A translation of Wynne-Edwards' grand

theory might be that the youth dimly realize and
resent the fact that they are no longer individually
unique, but a mass cliché. But to escape from the cliché
is the life-function of every individual, and it must
be done alone, not in a mob.

The current children's cant can be understood best
as a set of alibis in metaphor: "cool," "groovy," "bag,"
"uptight" (passionate or frustrated—a suggestive para-
dox), "loving spoonful" (heroin), "like" (preposition
both emphasizing and deemphasizing what follows),
"freak out," "soul brother," "scene" (stage center),
"where it's at" (scene). These terms are probably
ephemeral, and not worth noticing. Interestingly, most
of them can be used as evasive justifications of misbehavior; they have neurosis written all over them.
They escape into the locked room of the self, where
the cliché is a signal not only to others but more immediately to one's own dementia. This is the classic and
deadly cliché, the one that excludes the rest of the
world. Lenin and Hitler understood it perfectly, but
they turned it to positive uses. "Kill the landlords" or
"Kill the Jews" tried to justify the misbehavior. But
the children's clichés are only negative and impotent
apologies.

Why should one ask children to compete with Lenin
and Hitler? By the very nature of childhood, the children's cliché has no future. These trees are deciduous,
and shed their leaves at the first frost.

Sociologists who have forgotten they were ever
children justify the children's revolt by pointing to
"the failure of success," as achieved by the bourgeois
fathers. More delicious nonsense has rarely been
drooled. These fathers have obviously been good pro-

viders, probably too good. They have not been guilty of the much more traumatic "failure of failure." A child must be grateful for a successful father. The failure is elsewhere, perhaps with the sociologists.

Material success may have its ignominious aspects, but success is where one finds it, as the child will later discover. Yet on this slogan of the "failure of success," the youthful minority presumes to downgrade achievement, excellence, security, the learning process, experience, education, democracy, and the Bill of Rights.

The youthful protests are indeed having their effect, and it is already visible. It is the breakdown of the long-term American aspiration for universal education. The respect for the school and the teacher has collapsed in some groups. Parents have come to agree with the youthful demand that education be unalloyed fun. In consequence, teachers are flocking away from the disorderly schools, or leaving the profession entirely. Legislatures are cutting down educational grants. Benefactors are reducing endowment contributions.

The children's cliché ultimately runs into the hard fact that nobody, not even a child, can unilaterally demand anything. He cannot even demand that the one who knows, the teacher, share his knowledge. The peremptory child will get teachers as ignorant as himself, and then a little later those schools will stop the nonsense and close up. School standards can be lowered, but the universe cannot be persuaded to lower its standards. The youthful protests boil down to an objection to submitting to education at all. In that sense they will be successful.

Shocking as all this may sound, it makes excellent sense to a tiny minority of revolutionary youth. These children want power as obsessively as Lenin and Hitler wanted it. Certain leaders have informed them that democratic societies are too satisfied materially for old-style revolution. The only possible answer for the revolutionist is to shift the masses' aspirations away from everything material, sensible, and human, and toward something lunatic, which these ambitious boys have not yet been able to invent. But still the boys' glands tell them: *I need a revolution. I will think of something.* Talk now; think later.

It is not particularly the Establishment that they mean to destroy. It is instead the dignity of man, the essential illusions, the webs of communication, the social cements, for only if these are destroyed can the boys march over the debris of man to victory. One sound tactical approach to this end is to destroy the universities and universal education. Eventually the result would be retrogression to the rabble of the eighteenth century, ripe for revolution. (I had this idea thirty-eight years ago, published it, and forgot it.)

But the boys want something quicker; they can nearly taste their victory. If only they could introduce LSD to their whole generation, everybody would realize that there are better things in life than food, shelter, babies, love, and everything any sane human lives for. In that cuckooland, revolution might be possible. The glorious incoming generation that these leaders envisage is one unanimously hooked on the more advanced drugs. With this synthetic proletariat, they think they might accomplish something great. For them. Not for the people, God, no! The people are hopeless. For this would be a revolution *against* people.

But this is lunatic and impossible. The apparent must be apparition. One might consider the possibility that the children are dancing to a music they do not hear. But history remembers such a music.

Earlier civilizations often acknowledged the orgiastic drives in mankind, which are conspicuously not accommodated by modern Western civilization. A serious competitor of early Christianity under the Roman Empire was the belief in Cybele, Great Mother of the Gods, and her consort Attis, and her demonic Corybantes. This cult gloried in wild dances to a din of flutes, tambourines, cymbals, castanets, and frenzied screaming, accompanied by self-mutilations. The priests were long-haired eunuchs dressed as women. Attis symbolized the flowers of spring. The faithful adored both love and horror.

The children's cliché may then be seen as an attempt to revive these perennial orgiastic compulsions. Even if they have never heard of Cybele, it is suggestive that they have adopted the forms of her worship.

Seen purely as pagan glorification of the orgiastic, a long-haired college riot with screaming, flowers, and ordure can be understood, perhaps with sympathy. But because the boys do not know what they are doing, they cripple the effect by insisting that the riot has a secular rationale. (Down with the new gymnasium or the U.S. Department of Defense or ROTC.) The words do not march with the music. The ritual frenzy peters out in slogans.

This disproportion between music and words may explain the travesty or transvesting of the children's cliché. It is not a revolution; it aspires to be a religion.

In this vein a small cadre of youth revolted at

Columbia University in the spring of 1968, forcibly
occupied buildings, injured custodians and police, stole
and burned official and scholarly papers, set fires, broke
windows, threw their ordure out the windows, and
demanded—that is the word—perfect amnesty. Their
leader, an apish youth named Mark Rudd (the name
produces the sound, Crudd), son of a retired lieutenant
colonel and a doting mother, delivered to the president
of the university this declaration: "If we win, we will
take control of your world, your corporation, your
university." Somebody should have laughed, and kept
on laughing. For it was not the president's or the
trustees' or the faculty's university to give or keep.

A university is owned by the whole society, and is
legally treated in that light. Columbia's endowment
of $300 million or so cannot be suddenly divided up
among the trustees or the administration or the faculty
or the alumni, and not by a Cruddish committee. A
university is a charitable institution, protected by laws
and checks and balances from looting, and offering an
education that nobody wholly pays for. It is "owned,"
if at all, by anybody who helps it. Since it invites
strangers into its purlieus, it is peculiarly vulnerable to
riot by the befriended, just as a church would be, or
a hospital, or a breadline. Rudd was only a bum on a
breadline who had the neanderthal idea of wrecking
the soup-kitchen. At its most brilliant, this exemplifies
the thinking of the youth (which Jimmy Durante
always pronounced "yute").

Part of the job of running Columbia University is
managing that $300 million. Rudd's committee would
have had to assume this farcical responsibility, or just

grab the liquid assets and run. The second alternative is the better.

The proper reaction to a Rudd is laughter—while throwing him out into the street, but laughingly. The "anguished reassessments" of the Columbia administration, and the semantics of the flap-brained sector of the Columbia faculty reveal that they do not know when to laugh, possibly disqualifying them from dealing with youth at all.

A preposterously serious discussion appeared, in *The New York Times Magazine* of May 26, 1968, of just how people like Rudd could help run a great university. All that one can really say is that tyrannical decisions by faculty and administration might properly be brought into the open and adjudicated. As an undergraduate, I suffered a number of these, and fought back as an individual, not as a riot. When I defied the administration as an eighteen-year-old, what really shocked me was that these grown men took me seriously, and that I could lecture them on morality. If any of them had just laughed, I would have kept some of my illusions about my elders.

Grant that American universities can be improved. The appropriate philosophers to study the matter would hardly seem to be a rabble of riotous youths who hate the university. Better to find adults who know the whole evolution of universities; the specific history of American schools; the particular university to be reformed; the enormous expansion and fragmented specialization of human knowledge; the obligations of the sciences and the humanities to the people, the government, and even industry; and some sophisticated philos-

ophy of what young people need to know and how to
get it into their heads. One may doubt whether such
people exist but if they do, they will not be nineteen
years old, long-haired, bearded, unbathed.

There is still more to the university equation. In his
book *The American University,* Jacques Barzun lists
some of the current university functions: free clinics,
legal aid, business advice, slum clearance, real estate,
foreign exchange students, scholarships, job procure-
ment, student counseling, psychiatric help, publications
and radio stations, military draft records, an enormous
increase in courses and teachers because of specialization, night courses, remedial courses, community relations, observatories, oceanographic research, tropical
medicine institutes, fund-raising, and alumni relations.

One Draconian reform would be to abolish all
services except teaching and research, obliging each
student to solve his own problems in his own way,
including room and board. This would stun the Rudds
into perfect silence. The university would thus have
ceased to be a surrogate parent indulging revolt, and
become a store selling education. Just show up and
pay for it, get it, and go away.

Of the *soi-disant* revolutionary young, I sense that
they have no burning curiosity about the past, that is,
no real desire to be educated. But the past is an exciting and certifiable part of the present and future. If
a boy does not know that Descartes existed, he is still
only a boy, even in long pants and a long beard. If
he does not know about Plato, the beard should be
longer.

One might justly expect the young to be searching
for some higher happiness than other generations have

found. But it is the universal observation that these young are not happy, and do not want to be happy. Since they are all trying to be individuals, they hate one another; they stalk about like a pack of cats in a backyard, tails lashing, while they prattle of love, a love that radiates out into the stratosphere and may influence some distant planet, but nothing on this planet. They have sworn off joy, even such small joys as taking a hot shower or shaving, or, if female, smelling good or looking good or having clean hair. Whether they are grateful for a beautiful day, I do not know. Whether the males are grateful for a beautiful woman, I doubt.

Nor have they discovered asceticism, which might justify their disdain of happiness and joy. The groveling pose might be understandable in such a lazarland as India but it is preposterous in America. It has a logic: The white youth want to shame their parents; the black youth want to shame their race. Bless them both, but they have failed. Though dismayed, the proud whites and blacks go their way, not without sorrow.

One evidence of thought is visible. We have "the politics of participation," a grisly and wildly satirical understatement for rioting, booing, and presumably assassination, but not for voting. Participation it is, and the wonderful thing is that the participants can see some results immediately, and sometimes see themselves later on TV reruns.

It took some time for the youth to attract serious examination when it was discovered that the combination of private debauchery and public revolutionary idealism was not in line with doctrinaire traditional patterns, as expressed by Hus, Luther, Robespierre,

Marx, Lenin. It is more appropriate to study these
youth superficially, for they are all surface. They
have earned a laugh, no more, not a large laugh.

The vapidity is such that one could exhilarate them
by suddenly bursting into song, with:

> Abide with me! Fast falls the eventide,
> The darkness deepens. Lord, with me abide!
> When other helpers fail, and comforts flee,
> Help of the helpless, oh, abide with me!

In fact, the whole culture is loaded with such gems,
of which they are merely ignorant.

The conceit of these people is that they are Outlaws.

Let us consider the Outlaw in man. It is held in check
for long periods, as under the Roman Empire, the
feudal system, the Pax Britannica. The Outlaw was
suddenly loose when the Vikings discovered that they
could loot the rubble of the Roman Empire and riot
at will, until they were subdued several centuries later
by the feudal system. (That was a long riot.) In recent
times Communism, now the most ruthless enemy of the
Outlaw, has still given several demoralizing examples
of how to uproot traditional social orders with a few
choice clichés. Before Communism, Anarchism, virtually devoid of usable ideas, was bewitchingly attractive. For the image of the Outlaw is always magnetic
to a surprisingly large number of people (except its
victims). The current youth were surpassed in the
eighteenth century by Englishmen who rejoiced in
the secret midnight Black Mass, and again in the nineteenth century.

The Outlaw today, complete with the long hair of the

wild North Ireland clans, is an insipid parody of the sixteenth century.

The defense against the eternal Outlaw is to prove that there is something worth preserving and somebody who is resolved to preserve it. For the Outlaw is inherently frivolous; he wants to have some fun and get something for nothing; the mania, devoid of ideas, is short-lived if it encounters the virtues of continuity, calm, and courage.

It is interesting that the Outlaw does not arise in primitive societies. There, the Outlaw is simply recognized as crazy; he is killed or commits suicide. The Outlaw seems therefore a luxury of more advanced societies. Perhaps the point is that the current children shame the good name of Outlaw.

But no; they are pseudo-Outlaws whose invariable recourse is the practical joke, a form of malice formerly perfected by the English and Australians. Now it has reached American youth under the label of "put-on." The youth at Berkeley, at Columbia, at the Chicago Convention were acting out a practical joke, while playing puppets to more serious people who were, in effect, playing a practical joke on them. Anybody is vulnerable to a practical joke—once. (Both the youth and the Chicago police must have learned something.) The interlocking practical jokes had to be played out with a straight face, and so they were, to the end. Since the Establishment finds it very difficult to laugh, it did not laugh.

Lunatic ideas put into effect—such as the ideas of Lenin, Mussolini, Hitler, Stalin—may well be characterized as practical jokes, for certainly somebody laughs, if it is only the Devil. In this sense, one can understand the new amateur jokers, the youth who pretend to be the Red Guard or the *Sturmabteilung*. And why not? It's a joke. They are the Kronstadt sailors of 1917. Why not? It's a joke. Or they are Che Guevara, heroically showing themselves on the streets of American cities. Why not? It's a joke. Or they are good old Ho-ho-ho, gambling that he won't get hit with an atom bomb. Ho-ho-ho, it's a joke. We should understand that the models for very large practical jokes have been given the children, and that these have a record of having worked.

But the children have not understood the models. If one walked down the street wearing the awesome badges of the Orders of the Bath, Teutonic Knights, Garter, Elephant, Pour La Mérite, Golden Fleece, and Holy Sepulchre, nobody would understand the joke, and it would remain in a vacuum. The youths' practical jokes, particularly in their *avant-garde* costumes, tend to suffer from the same failure.

The hoodlum, as distinguished from the true Outlaw, has always existed in a majority of the youth. The present youth apparently do not dare to operate as individual, unregimented hoodlums; they are organized, like the Sicilian Mafia. The true hoodlums today exist only in prisons, or are on their way there. Interestingly, the true hoodlums in the prisons were unanimously contemptuous of the young rioters in Chicago, and sided with the Chicago police. For a convict doing twenty years for bank robbery knows instinctively his difference from exhibitionists or *provocateurs*. He just breathes in, and he smells the difference. He took a risk; these others are making small jokes.

The present youth's uproar is primarily motivated by terror at the prospect of passing into that middle area between youth and age when one must meet life for the first time. For the young are really as jealous of their elders' age as the elders are jealous of the young's youth, health, and beauty. They overcompensate for this jealousy by imagining that any thought they have is the wisdom of the ages. There are many things these thinkers do not know. One is that they will eventually die. But they are immortal, and the immortal have no need of a sense of humor.

The eighteen-year-olds are certain that they are the end of the line, the ultimate heirs of all the millennia. They have forgotten the two-year-olds. Youth has indeed a nonnegotiable enemy against which it must immediately riot. It is time. For the clock is ticking away their youth, without recourse.

~§ 10 §~

The Instant Celebrity
Cliché

Conditioned by the media, especially TV, the children have all seen the vision that they will all, each and every one, somehow become a celebrity, certainly not by arduous effort, but by some magic of the mysterious self. They have come to think that the electric circuit from childish nonentity to world fame can be instant, lighting up the whole horizon. Yes, indeed.

At the lowest level, the vision is completed by youths mugging old ladies, perhaps raping and killing them, for such deeds certainly elevate the individual youths out of considering themselves as part of the dull commonalty of mankind. If they are not caught, the celebrity is at least in their own minds, and of course they tell their friends about their heroism, gaining prestige.

The same vision appears to college students in college riots who disport themselves for the TV cameras often under the direction of the TV cameramen. If their parents, who were really paying for them to be educated, see them on TV, they are instant celebrities. Instant celebrity is well worth a degree.

The Negro jokers compete in the expression of lunacies to get into the instant celebrity business. They seem to come and go. The older men remain.

Boy and girl singers are frequently instant celebrities, some millionaires while still adolescent.

The assassins of public figures, if they are caught, are instant celebrities.

Any professor who can assassinate the good record of the United States has an instant following.

Most current art is only a play for instant celebrity, and those who understand this clearly get rich.

If the road to success had suddenly become easy and instant, we would soon be blessed with 40 million rampant celebrities. But the rest of us, the essential audience for a celebrity, cannot remember the names of 40 million simultaneous celebrities. The 39,999,900 who are automatically crowded out immediately go into a tantrum, crying: *me, me.* Even the ones who become instant celebrities, such as Barbra Streisand, seem to be crying: *me, me.* And again Andy Warhol: *me, me.* And again Allen Ginsberg: *me, me.*

The concept of instant celebrity is miraculous but its parentage is very ordinary and familiar. It is simply the electronic and deformed version of the Horatio Alger story, which was formerly the miraculous, liberating pride and hope of successive waves of American immigrants. The fathers and grandfathers of the magical youth are frequently Horatio Alger success stories. (Somebody look up the parentages of Streisand, Warhol, Ginsberg, but not me, me.) But these youth have looked at the Horatio Alger story and when they noticed that it involved hard work, discipline, self-denial, they fled from it. Worst of all, it took too long. These children cannot wait. If the bathroom is a minute away, they must do it in the diaper. This is their thing.

The children's answer is that all the tedium, the waiting, even the trip to the bathroom, the self-discipline, the sense of mastery of oneself and so of mastery of the medium, can all be eliminated, and thus celebrity gained at one spastic leap or one catatonic fit.

Let me help. At least a local instant celebrity can be gained in an infinity of ways. One can simply use an obscene word in polite ("square") company, pin a general's five stars on each shoulder, climb a telephone pole, ride on top of an automobile, hang an effigy of somebody from one's front window, wear the American flag, burn the American flag (a suggestion: burn the Confederate flag), wear a coat of many colors with miscellaneous bijouterie, dye the hair green or orange, sleep on a platform in a tree, paint ZOWIE! on the side of one's car, set up as a *guru* (not difficult), inflate one's breasts (if female) with injections of silicone emulsion, be a really terrible bore or nag, or commit suicide in an unusual way, as by guillotine.

We are more accustomed to the three youths who call themselves the Dead Hands and produce a musical blat more painful to the ear than the last electronic caterwaul, and are soon rich. But for the millions who cannot do even this, a sort of street celebrity may be attained by clothing and, for the boys, a topiarian cultivation of head and face hair, and, for the girls, painting the eyelids and lips unnatural colors. As the heads turn, instant celebrity!

If nature has denied one the right to look splendid, there remains the right to look repulsive.

Both are desirable, for these people are thinking like actors: they are looking for juicy roles, whether as hero or heavy. The world is the stage they're on; real life is inconsequent and far away on the street outside the theater which they never leave.

One artist strewed a vacant lot with pieces of trash and promised to remove numbers of them day by day, thus producing a dynamic, progressive art work as the trash disappeared. This gentleman was simply inviting people to play with him in a game he had invented. Instant celebrity.

One can walk through museums of modern art, if one is looking for significant beauty, at a dead run, as I do. The pictures on display are inviting one to play little games with them. First they say, I'll bet you can't figure out the rules of this game; then they say, You lose. But I have never seen any occasion to play another man's game. Games are easy; beauty is difficult. Somebody must have noticed that the beauty of the "Mona Lisa" and the "Virgin of the Rocks" is mysterious, and glibly hypothesized that anything that is mysterious is beautiful. The perfect way to be mysterious is to be meaningless: the cipher with no solution. The pointless game.

Art works by instant celebrities, costing millions of dollars, become worthless even as we look at them, sucked into the retreating tide of garbage. One prays that the "in" people who bought them can make them tax-deductible.

The young hero, or the genius who proves his powers early, is oddly exhilarating to nearly everybody, even to the old failures. The great mathematicians, Archimedes, Newton, Euler, Gauss, Galois, Einstein, *et al.*, ennoble all men everywhere. The expression, "the marvelous boy," describing Chatterton, an unusual youth who died quickly (arsenic), as did Galois (duel), tells us that youth can be marvelous. Its application to the instant celebrities turns it into a degrading cliché. The young celebrity becomes a bore, who refuses to go away when he gets older. The cultural sewers are clogged with decaying instant celebrities for whom no dissolvent has yet been marketed.

True, the sewers are usually small sewers, as of one block or one cellar, for the celebrity had never been visible to more than five or twenty or a hundred other people.

But, to be fair, the youth may be in tune with larger rhythms in the society than the square adults realize. At the highest levels of corporate industry, instant celebrity is regarded as the short road to riches. The so-called glamour stocks are touched with this magic. Of one sort are the "conglomerates" where fiendish accountants juggle the assets of a dozen operations, real and imaginary, into a sky-filling aurora borealis. More important are the firms asociated with the military establishment, which in turn is necessarily associated with the enormous tax income. These, like the young singing millionaires, have refined instant celebrity into a golden alchemy. For example, of thirteen electronic systems built for the Air Force and Navy, nine, costing a total of $115 billion, were worthless; the other four, costing $5 billion, were of some use. As a rule the companies making the worthless systems tended to make more money than those making the useful systems, as one might have begun to suspect.

These revelations were contained in a report entitled "Improving the Acquisition Process for High Risk Military Electronic Systems." General Dynamics, a notably glamorous firm, had a perfectly splendid earnings record while producing seven weapons systems, none of which "measure up to expectations." Not measuring up to expectations is a way to get rich that differs from the Horatio Alger story in a way that must delight the youth. It is also customary for electronic systems to cost two to three times as much as expected, and to be produced two years late. Delightful!

The dud systems are commonly the product of heroic "crash" programs undertaken in haste to achieve significant "breakthroughs." "Crash" and "breakthrough" are terms congenial and indeed intoxicating to any youth at any time. They promise instant celebrity, if only one touches with one finger the right spot and the whole pretense crashes and everybody breaks through.

The report for "Improving the Acquisition Process" offers the solution that no single firm be given responsibility for a "crash" program but that at least two companies try to "crash" in parallel, thus perhaps restoring to the Pentagon the old simplicities of competition, incentive, economy, efficiency, and even results.

But these are precisely the simplicities that the instant celebrity youths—and the Pentagon?—propose to eliminate from their careers. They dream of a marvelous life of no competition, no incentive, no economy, no efficiency, no results. The Pentagon has nearly achieved the dream; the youth are still dreaming. Certainly they are both spoiled. Still, the youth do not throw away $115 billion just to show off, though they undoubtedly would if they had it.

What we have seen in the past thirty years is a paroxysm of human arrogance among businessmen, scientists, generals, now reaching even to women, children, Negroes, and homosexuals, so that they all see visions of miracles without effort. The Declaration of Independence, it would seem, promised them all instant celebrity. As the jubilance of the Fools' Festival rises, something else mounts—it is called pollution: sewage-clotted rivers, sulphured and carbon-dioxided air, vast garbage dumps and car cemeteries, pesticide-poisoned fauna, LSD- and amphetamine-poisoned children. Pollution has become a part of the culture for the polluted. Since the clichés of instant celebrity can readily be included in the list of pollutants, their devotees must be described as polluted. But why be kind? They are in fact pollution.

Anybody who describes America as a "sick society" is pollution, rather than polluted, but he can be sure of an instant celebrity, notably in the colleges. Instant celebrity thus becomes a synonym for instant pollution.

❦ 11 ❧

The Electronic Man
Cliché

Novel ideas, if sufficiently obvious, have a singular
appeal in this immediate period. Surely nudity, obscenity, the universality of bodily functions, the female
legs exposed by the miniskirt have all been obvious
realities for thousands of years. Everybody knew that
the female of the species had complete legs from foot
to hip; everybody knew about pubic hair; everybody
knew that everybody else did the same things one did
oneself.

The fate of these novel and obvious ideas is to
become almost immediately clichés. When it became
clear that the female leg, a cardinal attraction for many
centuries, was merely what kept the female mobile,
it lost most of its interest. The so-called dirty words
became clichés without force.

A subtler novel idea, which is still fairly obvious, is
that all modern men and women have been changed in

nature by their habitual use of tools, especially electric and electronic devices: TV, telephone, elevator, automobile, airplane, and so on. It is said that the new generation, which is accustomed to these tools, is utterly different from all the generations of man, and that people past some stated age are obsolete. Intellectuals who are easily bullied by novel ideas write seriously of an electronic or technological or "extended" man, or youth, as if God had whipped up a new creation. These intellectual sycophants have pawned their souls for the cliché.

The way to fight one's way out of the cliché is, first, to relax, and then to look at what actually goes on.

The elevator stops at the fifteenth floor because a man there has pressed a button. He enters and presses the button marked 1. The elevator descends, in electronic response, as the lights above flash 14, 13, 12, etc. He falls fourteen stories under control and exits safely at the first floor. The electronic man, haha.

Can anybody suppose that he has an absolute faith in this machine, that he does not know that it has an innate capacity to kill him and no innate objection to doing so? The machine runs by laws of its own, which have nothing to do with him, and he knows it. The machine is totally different from his animal self; to pretend that it is a marvelous new member of his body, enabling him to drop fourteen floors in safety, is an insult both to him and to the elevator.

All machines fail (I have been in a free-falling elevator), and as long as people keep that knowledge, they cannot become the electronic man. They will remain intelligent animals immune to the electronic cliché, and have some hope of survival. If they step into an elevator that isn't there, they will try to grab a cable and slide down, as a desperate animal. The electronic man, who really believes in the machinery, will soon be eliminated.

The animal humans will also respect an electric light socket, gas range, automobile, airplane, telephone wire, and such lists always add the atom bomb, which as sentient and suspicious animals they must sense and suspect. These threats have only added to, not replaced, the more ancient terrors of lightning, cyclone, fire, flood, earthquake, volcanic eruption, blizzard, and for prehistoric man, the cave bear.

The natural terrors are real and eternal, except for the cave bear. Death by automobile or airplane is real enough, but it is a side-effect of an exclusively human game of rapid transit, and it will cease in any society that cannot afford the automobile and airplane. It is absurd to say that a man in a plane is moving at supersonic speed. He is not moving at all; the plane is moving, and he is being carried. He is being carried much faster, in fact, as a passenger on the planet Earth, which is both revolving around the Sun and being whirled through space as part of this solar system. No passenger on the Earth thinks of himself as a superb space-traveler; a passenger on a plane is equally involuntary, once the plane is in the air.

The novel idea is that the electronic and technological devices have absolutely changed the contemporary and future man into something unrelated to the animal kingdom. After all, what other Earth animal goes to the moon? Surely the youths born with these powers will hatch out of the pupae of their parents

and take wing as imagos of a new creation, something
more than man.

Some of the youths actually believe it, and fly on
LSD and the other de-animalizing drugs. By repetition,
the non-animal novel idea has become a cliché. For it
is really a very old idea. Formerly, man's animalism
was definitively abolished by the concept that he had
a soul and a reasonable hope of an afterlife. No animal,
he. Like the soul, electronics absolutely separates man
from the apes, and we have done it again. We are
Special. The electronic cliché is the new soul. The prin-
cipal priest of the new religion is Marshall McLuhan,
who is certainly known to all. And it is indeed a religion. For the youths discovered that the way for an
animal to *feel* electronic was to take drugs. Feeling one
with God used to be a difficult achievement; feeling
supersonic on drugs is automatic. The new religion
tends to destroy the true believers. They cease to be
mere animals; instead, they are demented or dead. As
the price of piety, this must seem excessive.

But suppose the youth grow up and realize that they
prefer to be animal? Anybody can choose. When the
music jangles his nerves, he turns it off. When the
television bores him, he turns it off. He is alone in a
non-electronic room, looking into the silence. Billions
of unheard sounds, unseen pictures, flow past him into
the darkness, and he is again an animal and a man.

The idea that electronic man is more than man is
based on the reasonable metaphor that a tool of man's
is an extension of the physical man. McLuhan has
atrociously improved the metaphor by adding that the
extended member has been amputated by the tool.
For example, the wheel, elevator, plane, space capsule,

extend—and amputate—the feet. Without feet, this monstrous man can move at 800 mph, leap to the top of an eighty-story building, hop 5,000 miles or, in the case of astronauts, 240,000 miles, without working up a sweat.

Certainly, with his machines, this is a powerful man. These extraordinary abilities, incidentally, reduce to nearly zero his ability to look at the scenery in transit, and increase the number of places he has "been to" in a year or a lifetime. The process also increases his boredom with new places, even the moon, not to speak of Las Vegas, even as it theoretically refines his sophistication in choosing the final place to stop. In practice, this last turns out to be Florida or Southern California.

When he comes to a full stop he discovers, without any particular amazement, that he still has feet. The philosopher's grand insight that the vehicle had amputated his feet, it seems, was only a metaphor. But no surgeon includes among his tools the metaphor.

The electronic cliché always has this strain of incantation, of unilateral magic spells that bewitch only zombies. If somebody tells me that various of my members are now amputated and unusable, am I permitted to tell him which of his members are amputated and unusable? Or would this be only tennis or pingpong?

For we are further told that the mind of the literate man is absolutely crippled by reading the printed word which runs in a linear or sequential arrangement (as on this page), one word plodding after the other, the sequence arbitrarily broken by the width of the page, naturally broken by the syntax of the sentences, but all in a series of lines running, in English, from left to right and from top to bottom, and so to the next page, numbered sequentially. Linear. This is very bad.

Why it is bad is not clear. The jargon is that it makes the reader detached, objective, informed, factual, unemotional, unsuperstitious, activist, executive, opinionated, time-conscious, habituated to a subject and a predicate, a noun and a verb, one thought at a time, one thing at a time, that is, in sum, "hot" as opposed to "cool." It cannot be claimed that my mind (the first person is obligatory here) runs from left to right or from top to bottom, or even that its operations are linear or sequential or most of the other adjectives given just above. The adjectives radial, meandering, groping, experimental, haphazard, intuitive, reckless, or irresponsible would probably be more appropriate to the process, in my case. The shape of the resultant mind might be an icosahedron, certainly not a square.

To return to the cliché, we are told that Gutenberg's invention of alphabetic type and print amputated the individual's sense of participation. In fact, since everybody read substantially the same words, if they read at all, they were all suddenly in agreement, and out of this unanimity emerged the European nations of the sixteenth century, ending the chaos of feudalism. Participation.

Something is seriously askew in the cliché. Reading obviously heightens the sense of participation with something, outside the room, perhaps outside the nation. The participation is complete if everybody reads the same words. But soon a great variety of words became available, and whole peoples ceased to think in perfect unison. These readers were still participating, but in different things, even in the same room. Both

Henri IV and Emperor Charles V believed that Christian Europe could be united, but there were already too many different words, too much participation in different beliefs.

And during the next four centuries this was the state of the Western world before any of the so-called "cool," meaning vague, blurred, media arrived.

The definition of a "cool" medium is that the receiver of the message knows that he has received a message, but cannot define what the message was. A better description of a cliché can hardly be perfected. The "cool" media are identified as cartoon, newspaper item, telegraph, telephone, jazz, and television. With rare exceptions, these media convey vague, blurred messages to the receivers, which they would be hard put to define in hard, hot, linear words.

One can see that people who are exposed and respond only to "cool" cliché messages might begin to differ from civilized people who read. This group, whose individuals are atomized, whose thinking faculty is disabled, whose response to the clichés is instinctive, must be compared to a cloud of dancing gnats. They are ready for dictatorship.

It is nearly a punishable indictment of Marshall McLuhan that he does not point out this elementary fact. But perhaps he wanted a few modest months of power first himself.

Already the mindless, unanimous dance of the midges is what we see around us in the agitation of the children. The cloud vibrates nervously, tirelessly, in anticipation of the dictator. It awaits the grand master who will lead the dance. The New Left is merely a school of larval dictators; certainly one of them must burst into the imago which will lead the swarm into the fire.

It is still a small swarm. For the majority of the youth, the "generation gap" is a myth. They communicate more easily with their elders today than at any other time within my knowledge.

The crude prediction is made that in a "cool" world civilized citizens of large nations will retrogress into members of local primitive tribes. Tribalism already covers most of the Earth's surface, notably in Africa and Asia, especially north of the Kun Lun Mountains, including Turkestan and the Taklamakan and the great tribes to the north, occupying the veritable "heartland" of Eurasia. Whether tribalism will break up large civilized nations is open to doubt.

Should the "cool" media ever enlist the mass of Americans into the swarm of dancing gnats, it might be predicted that the swarm would conquer Canada and Mexico and all Latin America, and dance on until it had destroyed itself. The orders to the dancing gnats would all be clichés, perfectly understood by the swarm, but indefinable in linear words. "All men are proletarians" or "Germany ought to be great" are not linear statements; they are imprecise, radial clichés. One could reply: Who said I'm a proletarian? or, How great should Germany be? But when the "cool" clichés are all, nobody will reply. The vague, blurred message will throb on every air, in every brain: Proletarianproletarianproletarian, or, Germany—or America—ought to be greatgreatgreatgreat. All the gnats will be totally absorbed dancing to the cliché, Greatgreatgreatgreatgreat. A convulsion of rage would pass through the swarm, should they suddenly hear a voice saying: What do you mean by great? Great in what specific ways? How great? Why great at all? What would be in it for me? The questions would jar the beautiful rhythm of the demented dance, and in the trauma of the swarm, the voice would be destroyed.

This phenomenon, horrible as it is, is not a fantasy. On a small scale, we see it in the beats-hippies-yippies-crazies who impose on their members the happily accepted tyranny. Their description of the tyranny is that they have all thought their way into all the other minds, but this merely means that they have all reduced themselves to a gross common factor, which must be a cliché. Clichés will always drive individual ideas off the market. In the end, the cliché-master must take charge, and so he will.

The electronic swarm must abolish everything that is linear or sequential. This would naturally eliminate clocks, by which four o'clock comes after three o'clock comes after two o'clock, for all the members of the whole society. It is now three o'clock. I know that I will be hungry at six o'clock. I can then estimate, from experience, how much I can do in the three hours between three and six. I know also that a restaurant, using the same time, will be ready for dinner at six o'clock. In those three hours I can luxuriate in time. The clock-conscious really own time; they *have* plenty of time. In this way, I can plan my sleeping time. And what is sleep but a wallowing in time? Without it, one dies.

Another electronic cliché is to be aware of everything simultaneously. On the walls of this room are six paintings and a terrain map of Europe. To be aware of them all at once, even if possible, would be chaotic, for very unequal talents are saying very different things. To look at them one at a time might be useful, but it would be linear.

At the elite levels of electronic youth there is an aspiration to explode and implode, with the aid of drugs and electronic lights and sounds, sometimes wonderfully ingenious. One can only comment that these poor bastards are still only animals. Their experiments culminated briefly in the so-called discothèque, which died for the "square" reason that the noise and lights were unbearable to any animal, even the electronic human. There were no rats in discothèques; they had fled.

The electronic simultaneity cliché is probably derived from the indubitable fact that in any animal body a great many things are always happening simultaneously, from the pumping heart and lungs to the sixty thousand miles of human capillaries, the tiny pituitary and hypothalamus glands, and the brain. This exquisitely synchronized orchestra can be described as electronic, but this is only a little semantic joke. Mammals have been here for 170 million years without benefit of electronics. The animal miracle is infinitely more awesome than any electronic masterpiece of man's. Shocking as it may sound, a space capsule is less remarkable than a mosquito. But just now, man is more fascinated by his own feats than by God's.

The electronic vision of simultaneity, reminding us of the instant celebrity cliché, may explain why the revolutionary youth and their junior faculty *gurus* do not know how to think. The poor fools think they're electronic. That omnidirectional simultaneity, the illusion of a dynamo wired in all directions, paralyzes any

rational powers they ever had. They cease to be verte-
brates and revert to the third phylum, to the sea anemones whose tentacles in fact exert an omnidirectional
simultaneity outward with stinging cells having the
practical purpose of catching prey. The youth and the
junior faculty have no such equipment and hence are
fake sea anemones, alas.

Great fallacies such as the electronic cliché are perfectly capable of becoming theologies. But the heart
of this theology exposes itself on the most trivial level.
We are told that the waltz and presumably also all the
other coupled dances are "hot" and bad, while the
twist, the separated strutting of male and female, is
"cool" and admirable. But in the coupled dance two
people collaborated in synchronized response to the
music and learned something about themselves and one
another. In the twist, one exhibits oneself to oneself
and learns nothing.

On this frivolous level, it is revealed that the god of
the theology is oneself. In such a theology drugs, mas-
turbation, homosexuality, lesbianism, narcissism must
be the elements of the sacrament. The great fault of
the god himself, who has no goal, no future, is that one
knows Him too well.

The technological revolution actually going on will
do better without the electronic man. It should not
discourage scientists, but might better inspire them,
to realize that a space capsule is less remarkable than
a mosquito. The technological revolution will not get
far if it is conceived as against the universe. It might
better be taken as a further fulfillment of the universe's
own plan, within finite bounds.

⋘ 12 ⋙

The Sex Cliché

The cliché against which the females are currently revolting, partly explicitly but largely unconsciously, is of course romantic love. This mystery was invented in the eleventh century by the troubadours of southern France and northern Italy, and was truly a new invention. Its dissemination was restricted to the aristocracy, who enjoyed it but did not permit it to influence their marriage arrangements, which continued to be based on land, money, and position. Only the intellectuals really believed in romantic love. But the idea had been planted in men's minds that a woman, a particular woman, could be a magical thing. At least Abelard and Dante thought so. In thinking so, they had exploded the primeval axiom that the human male and female are members of the same animal species. The male had somehow concluded that the female, in both a physical and a spiritual sense, was not a part of

114

the same creation as himself. Intercourse, so routine in other species, became more than a sacrament; it became a poem, but only to the male. This delightful separation of the species into two species generated much of the West's extravagant energy for nine hundred years and may have been the vital "secret of the West."

The energy was inspired in the males by the females. The female image was soft, kindly, graceful, delicate, defenseless, innocent, chaste, covered by an elaboration of unfunctional clothing given to bows, ribbons, flowers, feathers, and often wildly exaggerating the bosom and hips. All of what was hidden was magical in the desired female, but the unmentionable heart of the matter was of course the female groin, the seat of the clitoris, labia, vagina, and Scarpa's fascia. And the beautiful and practical consequence of arriving at this paradise was a baby.

Since the reality was conventionally unknown to the male until his wedding night, and was not objectively assessed for some further time, if ever, what he expected was a cliché. This was inculcated in him by every instrument of the culture. Simply by lying on her back the female was universally understood to make a gift more precious than coronets.

The propaganda machine for the cliché, the *idée reçue,* consisted of the most powerful and canonical expressions of Western belief. Consider a few of them:

> O thou art fairer than the evening air,
> Clad in the beauty of a thousand stars.

> For where is any author in the world
> Teaches such beauty as a woman's eye?

But love . . . gives to every power a double power.

But, soft! What light through yonder window breaks.
It is the east, and Juliet is the sun.

She was a phantom of delight.

Whenas in silks my Julia goes,
Then, then (methinks) how sweetly flows
That liquefaction of her clothes.

And for bonnie Annie Laurie, I'll lay me doun and dee.

Her beauty, fervent as a fiery moon,
Made my blood burn and swoon.

Christ, if my love were in my arms,
And I in my bed again!

O lyric love, half angel and half bird,
And all a wonder and a wild desire.

Preposterous as these descriptions may seem, most
civilized men in the West for a millennium saw at least
a particular woman in exactly this light, extended hom-
age to some other women, and granted most women a
courtesy respect. When the illusion was murdered by
the particular woman, the man need only conclude
that he had chosen the wrong woman, and the illusion
survived. The customary expression of this difficulty is,
"My wife doesn't understand me," which really means
that she cannot meet the cliché.

The poets are not entirely besotted. They actually
give as much space to death and the weather as to romantic love. And they admit the split (cliché: dichotomy) in the love relationship, as in "For God's sake
hold your tongue, and let me love" or "The most happy

marriage . . . would be the union of a deaf man to a blind woman." But these were small jokes. The romantic image still dazzled civilized men.

The emerging bourgeoisie quickly noticed this aristocratic luxury, particularly as indulged by the royal court and celebrated by the poets and novelists. Within their means, they adopted it. And so for several hundred years there flourished the love story whose main plot line was whether boy would get to embrace girl. This was a valid plot because it involved the conjunction, tremulously uncertain, of members of two separate species, who progressively discover how different they are, never, or rarely, how identical they are. Nobody except Stendhal, and then Freud, seriously discussed love.

The difficulties of a great many popular magazines and writers began when this plot gradually, really invisibly, withered into an anachronism.

For one party to the plot seceded. Marvelous to relate, it was the females who elected to repudiate the plot and the cliché of differentness. One might think that anyone glorified by the adoration in the quotations given above would cling perpetually to such divinity, at any cost.

But no. The ladies, or a significant minority of them, seem to have decided that the adoration was a swindle. They had noticed that they were forfeiting such substantial perquisites as the vote, education, jobs, independence, legal rights, mobility, and free access to the local saloon, for a dubious nimbus. The fraud, if so it was, was of course most irritating to the older and plainer females, less so to the young and nubile.

The revolt against the sex cliché had begun. Apart

from the suffragettes, it was most visible in the female's sudden participation in athletics, particularly bathing and swimming. Annette Kellerman brought in the one-piece suit well before 1920. It was a golden age, but secretly, for the young. The incidence of premarital sexuality probably doubled in the 1920s, and the revolution was complete. It has not further increased, according to all competent surveys. It has remained at a percentage constant ever since, though recently the sluttish age has dropped as low as it can physically go. The real breakthrough was completed by one generation of young females who at first had small interest in the doctrinaire revolution. As these females matured, the revolution became evolutionary for several decades, and the love story survived on sufferance. But on some basic level, the ladies had not yet begun to fight.

It is absurd to suppose that fashion designers or the females who accept their designs are acting in response to philosophical or psychological convulsions in the mass psyche. But some unconscious thrust in the females can be deduced with reason when great numbers of them accept a kind of covering that makes them ridiculous.

This stage of the revolution was ushered in by female pants. All previous female clothing had concealed a physical fact about the human female that pants crudely revealed. This is that the average female's pelvis and loins present an intimidating, if false, impression of power. They appear to mean business. The male, though of course far more effective, has a generally small pelvis; for him it is only a base from which his legs and shoulders work; for the female it is, in the geopolitical word, the heartland. And by God, the females decided to say so. When one has watched a thousand adipose behinds rowing away ahead of one, something has been lost forever, and one must guess that this disillusion is exactly what the females had in mind. Every such woman, pulling on tight pants over her hams, must have reflected that now she would go out and assassinate the male dream. For the human female is exquisitely conscious of the impression she is making. And I mean every woman of every shape, age, and stage of dissolution, except only the pathetic young, probably diseased, camp-followers of the new Bohemia. But along with these, in the more normal females' subscription to the designers' pants, we began to detect perhaps the confession of a psychic revolution against the men's nine-hundred-year-old cliché. The love story was dying.

But the females had not yet begun to fight. There still remained the sacrosanct cliché, noted earlier, that the heart of the mystery of the human female was the groin. By some process mysterious to me, the females decided to call their own bluff. There is nothing there, they said, there was never anything to hide. It is all inside. Look. And so came the miniskirt. The myth of nine hundred years was dissolved in a twinkling, and with it went the dream, and perhaps the enormous energy.

Granted, the human chasm between the two sexes may be absurd. Female wolves do not hunt in a particularly feminine way. Lionesses do not kill more sweetly than lions. The male and female porcupines can hardly be distinguished. Why should the human sexes make such a dramatic issue of their differentness? But this species long ago decided that it was more than animal. It has certainly become less than animal, for few humans, male or female, are as successful animals as the average wolf, or average cockroach.

In denying her femininity, the new female has made herself less sexual and more animal. A full half of her is visible; the rest is deducible; "undressing with the eyes" by the old lechers is superfluous. She declares that she is as sexless in her functioning as a female wolf. No longer when the light breaks in the window is it conceivable that "Juliet is the sun," or a "phantom of delight," or anybody for whom to "lay me doun and dee." The love story, alas, is dead.

The response of the young males to the female revolution was a model of the confused Pavlovian reflex. They didn't know what they were doing, or why, but they had to do something. They put on feminine clothes, let their hair grow long, wore earrings, fancy hats, necklaces, flowers, and tried to present themselves as soft, kindly, graceful, delicate, defenseless, innocent, and chaste. While virtually asking to be raped, some of them became homosexuals, as the perfect answer to the female revolution.

To the dismay of the present young, this glorious revolution is far from unprecedented. It is only a new form of PreRaphaelitism, "the Renaissance of the Spirit of Wonder" in the latter nineteenth century in England. This was paralleled in France by "the decadents" of Baudelaire and Mallarmé. The period went in for flamboyant dress and hairstyles and to some extent for drugs and a yearning for "the supernatural." It exploded with its degeneration into homosexualism and the Oscar Wilde trial. The comparison with the present seems so obvious that somebody must have made it somewhere.

The female part of the present revolution is, however, novel. The first impact of the female upper thighs revealed by the miniskirt was erotic to men conditioned to think of these areas as sailors thought of their home harbor lights, as the gates of pleasure. But after one has seen ten thousand thighs, the effect becomes classically chaste. One comes to imagine that the high-thighed female is about to take off on the hundred-yard dash, or march up to Thermopylae, or win her brown belt in karate, or join the terrible Dahomeyan regiments of women of the last century whose mission was to capture the enemy for torture and sacrifice. These are hardly sexual or romantic thoughts; in that sense the female revolution has succeeded.

A consolation remains. There will always be females content to be females and males content to be males. But even their relations will be altered by the female revolution.

When grand illusions die, there need be no services, obituaries, flowers, but displacements do take place in the total culture, perhaps invisible and perhaps taken as trivial. One such, which may be both and may be neither, is to be found in the advertisements of popular movies.

In 1938 the advertised stars of the movies were Katharine Hepburn and Ginger Rogers (*Stage Door*), Claudette Colbert (*I Met Him in Paris*), Greta Garbo (*Camille, Conquest*), Eleanor Powell (*Rosalie*), Lily Pons (*Hitting a New High*), Myrna Loy (*Man-Proof*), Jeannette MacDonald (*The Firefly*).

In one week in 1958 there were still Rita Hayworth (*Pal Joey*), June Allyson (*My Man Godfrey*), Anna Magnani (*Wild Is the Wind*), but more often the names were Montgomery Clift, Robert Mitchum, Marlon Brando, Kirk Douglas, Alec Guinness. These are not female names.

Today the grand victory of the female revolution is that the percentage of male to female headliners is about three to one. The female has ceased to be interesting. Usually the sole star is Dick Van Dyke, Paul Scofield, Dean Martin, Dirk Bogarde, Zero Mostel, James Garner, Cornel Wilde, James Mason, more or less in default, for these names certainly do not interest me. The unstarred ladies do not know what happened to them. They might whimper that the new scripts give the best parts to the men, and therefore the star billing. What they should say is that the old love story, whose major plot was the "winning" of the female, is all but obsolete. Apart from that, what the females do or do not do is uninteresting, and so the plots concern what the males do or do not do. The audience no longer looks forward to the vicarious conquest of the female star, at the conclusion of the titillating suspense.

What remains of the ancient female image? The residual star females are tomboys, comediennes, eccentrics, uglies (Barbra Streisand, Sandy Dennis, *et al.*), oddities whom only an odd man would want to "win." These are typical of the new females who boldly ram into males on the street and in the supermarket, in contacts that would have been inconceivable even five years ago.

Natural females such as Elizabeth Taylor and Sophia Loren know enough to take eccentric parts, or look odd. Many of the present females are just as beautiful and adorable as those of the past, but the magic has been stripped from them. The heroine is merely a member of the same species as the male characters, sans illusion, sans mystery, no "phantom of delight," no "fiery moon," no "lyric love." Good God, no.

Such is the obituary at last of the old cliché. Omit flowers.

⊷§ 13 §⊷

The Political Cliché

Various societies have decided that politics was a Bad
Thing and chosen instead a Man, namely Lenin, Mussolini, Hitler, and a dozen living dictators today. Their
destiny is despair and death, quickly or slowly. The
democracies accept politics as essential to social life,
complete with its clichés. The danger comes when the
politician becomes the cliché.

The American politician today seems to have ac-
quired the odor of the ambulance-chaser and the mor-
tician. This may have begun in Dallas in 1963 when
Lyndon Johnson was involuntarily an ambulance-
chaser and his fellow-Texans tried to be morticians to
President Kennedy. A wisp of pure evil, never identified by the press but vaguely sensed by the whole people, attached itself to the classic politician, and hence
to all politicians. The peculiar personality of Lyndon

Johnson, however history may rate it, burned an atrocious brand into the American people for five years until they screamed. The fact that this democracy deterred Johnson from any dream of such power as De Gaulle seized in France is a modest testament to the American form of government. The American people were waiting until he went away, but meanwhile the image of all politicians was discredited, and we must await a rebirth of our faith in—whom? Why, ourselves. It does not seem immediately imminent.

Five years of Lyndon Johnson may ultimately be assessed as a complex swindle of the American people arranged by cabals of blackhearted somebodies (now filed under Lee Harvey Oswald) and blackhearted Republicans (now filed under Goldwater). The black hats won, perpetuating Johnson, who put on the wide Texan white hat, and probably fooled somebody. When we have forgotten that wide Texan hat, perhaps politics will become respectable again.

The happy politician is liked by everybody; this is achieved in the South simply by saying "nigger." This politician is reelected for forty years and rules the Senate. In the North, the clichés are not so simple or effective. The politician must use a single cliché which will mean different, and palatable, things to different groups who will add up to a majority. Such clichés are "peace," "justice," "law and order," etc., for all of these are well beyond human reach, and will probably always remain so. Each group receives the cliché as referring to a painfully real situation in which it is trying to survive, and assumes that the politician knows about, and is concerned about, that situation. But the

politician, as he utters the cliché, translates the situation in his own mind into a cliché, and can thereafter
deal with it only as cliché, not as reality.

The politician must educate the public but, like the
magazines and the schools, he must do this well within
self-defined limits. He is not in the business of telling
all, nor of saying what he really thinks. This would ruin
him, and he is probably not as talented as the editors
and the professors.

In 1968 Senator Eugene McCarthy tried saying what
he really thought. He did not appear to care whether
anyone liked him. He was not collecting votes; he was
saying what he thought was true. The party hacks were
not amused. They were on far more serious business
than the truth: their careers and sinecures. And Mc-
Carthy faded like the Cheshire Cat.

The politician is mentally incapacitated, further, by
the fact that he must think about power, day and night.
His power base in the electorate is unreliable, and he
is at least on the fringe of the most powerful complex
ever developed. Under the American tax system, the
government is bloated with money. The disposal of all
that money infatuates American politicians, large and
small, as if they were Roman emperors. The Nero syn-
drome especially dominates Washington, notably in
the executive branches and the Southern-dominated
money committees of the Congress. Elected politicians
betray this sense of power; their statements are wonderfully smug: they are relatively close to all that money.
For the moment they are powerful, and, especially if
they are lawyers, they are cashing in.

Their professional clichés are an odd blend of self-
dramatization, insult, and evasiveness. Herewith a few:

CHANGE OF MIND. Agonizing reappraisal or reassessment.

COMPROMISER. Trimmer, pussy-footer.

CONFRONTATION. Eyeball to eyeball.

COUP. Power grab.

DISSIDENT. Mugwump.

EARNEST. Running scared.

EASY VICTOR. Shoo-in.

ERRAND BOY. Gopher (go for).

ELDER STATESMAN. High muckamuck, sachem, mover and shaker.

EXTREMIST. Lunatic fringe, little old lady in tennis shoes.

GOVERNMENT FUNDS. Public trough, pork barrel.

HARD FACTS. Crunch, nitty-gritty.

LIBERAL. Bleeding heart, do-gooder.

NO OPINIONS. Unifier.

PARTY HACK. Wardheeler, wheelhorse.

PEOPLE. Grass roots, sovereign power.

PREARRANGED DEMONSTRATION. Voice from the sewer.

PUPPET. Straw man, paper tiger, stalking horse.

RIOTS. Long hot summer.

SECEDE. Bolt, take a walk, go fishing.

SLOWLY. With all deliberate speed.

SMALL AUDIENCE. Whistle stop.

SPEAKING TOUR. Rubber chicken circuit.

STATE DEPARTMENT. Foggy Bottom, cookie-pushers.

SURPRISE VICTOR. Dark horse, sleeper.

TOO MUCH. Overkill.

VICTORY. Landslide, avalanche, after whirlwind campaign.

These are of course the jargon of the trade. The

clichés dispensed to the people are not so succinct. These latter are typically imprecise and evasive, sliding off the frontal realities of the real situations in an interminable spate of words delivered with smashing sincerity. Evasions of reality that sound like grappling with reality are not easy to compose, and deserve our awe.

For example, in 1968, atomic war was described as "direct confrontation between the nuclear powers." The danger of Negroes taking union jobs away from whites became "economic growth is the answer to job security"—a truly beautiful evasion. American imperialism could be avoided by "regional pacts" against Communist imperialism—an idea as substantial as pipe smoke. The answer to labor troubles was "improved grievance procedures and improved impasse procedures." Sure, sure. The speaker was not trying to educate the public. He had proved little more than that he had read the newspapers.

For the people the election was simple. There were two issues, Vietnam and the poor, meaning the Negroes, all Negroes, rich and poor, and nobody else. The candidates knew this very well.

VIETNAM. All candidates implied that they wanted to get out of Vietnam, one way or another, as quickly as possible. This was the cliché. None mentioned the obvious fact that in a real war one pursues the enemy to his capital and seizes the rulers (instead of halting at the Rhine and shaking one's finger at Hitler). None discussed why this had not been done. None explained that America had lost over thirty-five thousand men in a game, not a war.

The most idealistic candidate had to accept the abuse of pacifists, hippies, *et al.*, who dared to call South Vietnam's defensive war (aided by the United States) "immoral." How can self-defense be immoral? Is a hippie who tries to survive immoral? Of course the murderer is always more dedicated than his victim; he always wants to kill more intensely than the victim objects to being killed. But the idea that this dedication makes the killer more moral than his prey is the atrocious invention of these philosophers. And yet it has found spokesmen, such as Marcuse, in America and elsewhere.

The candidates did not debate with those Americans who regarded Vietnam as an American imperialist adventure. I am not so patient. Any reader who believes that American policy is to remain forever in Southeast Asia (as China or Russia would unquestionably do) is so sunk in depravity that he is advised not to read further in these pages. He needs another kind of help.

NEGROES. All the candidates agreed on "law and order," to be applied brutally by Wallace, firmly by Nixon, gently by Humphrey. And that, with an occasional bow to "justice," was the cliché discussion of the Negro matter. This hardly described the whole black-and-white situation in America.

The political cliché will come clear negatively, if an honest account of the black-and-white situation is given. It will then be obvious, paragraph by paragraph, what a politician cannot say publicly. The suppression of everything that follows is the political cliché.

The poison in the generally healthy American society is traceable to the disgraceful performance of the white

South, perhaps the worst losers in history, avenging themselves on the Negro. (This would get the speaker ostracized in the Congress by the Southern bloc, some of whom are decent men.)

This infection intimidated and demoralized even northern Negroes for about eighty-five years, so that they accepted inferior status, enjoyed blackface comedians, and rollicked in the ghettoes. They accepted their lot. And it is an axiom, known to all, that anybody who accepts his lot will get nothing better in this world. (This would deeply offend the Negro elite, particularly the black faculty of the Negro colleges.)

It was not the Negro who broke out of his psychic prison, unless we remember a lone colored lady in Alabama who was suddenly too tired to go to the back of the bus. Instead the liberal Northern whites, right up to the Supreme Court, told the Negro he was as good as anybody. (This would astonish followers of Marcus Garvey, A. Philip Randolph, Thurgood Marshall, *et al.*)

For a dominant majority to try to surrender its advantage over a large subordinate minority is certainly noble, but humanly unnatural. (This would outrage the liberals.)

In all human history, the attempt has never before been made. (This would sound like a total dismissal of the civil rights movement.)

Being unnatural and unprecedented, the mass elevation of the Negro is reluctant on the part of some whites and suspect in the eyes of most blacks. Since Negroes are not fools, they know that some whites don't really mean it, and some don't mean it at all. (This would be taken as inflammatory subversion.)

On the practical level, how many, and which, Negroes does one rotate into which positions in the society: policemen, mailmen, teachers, baseball managers, football quarterbacks, trustees, cashiers, congressmen, police chiefs, club members, union members, astronauts, generals, long distance runners, advertising models, editors? (This would annoy a lot of whites now in the jobs.)

A respectable Negro columnist has reproached white liberals for ever thinking about anything, such as American foreign policy, other than the Negro cause. His word was "infamous." Negroes propose removing from the English language such expressions as black art, blackball, black bottom, Black Death, black flag, Black Friday, blackguard, blacklist, blackmail, Black Maria, black widow, as insults to blackness. Black is beautiful, they say, but Black Beauty is remembered as a horse. (This would insult the Negro intellectuals, who call themselves "black" though most of them are caucasoid.)

The spectacular part of the "Black Peril" is the organization called the Black Panthers. Their bloodcurdling cries invite their extermination and terrify white hysterics. But knowledgeable blacks confide that their numbers in the whole United States are somewhere between 500 and 1,000, and that the black community rarely thinks of them. The black community may underrate them, but it is evident that the whole society overrates them. (This deflation of the Black Panthers would enrage the "law and order" crowd, and also the Black Panthers.)

The silent "Black Peril" in the northern cities consists of the poor devils, usually from the South, who are

unassimilable, despised by Northern black girls, rejected by the ghetto, and often involuntary outlaws.
An indication of their reaction is that a recent gradu-
ating class of a New York reformatory was exclusively
black. As they graduated, one could afford a thought
for their forgotten victims, maimed, dead, hospitalized,
hysterical, hobbling, most of them black, some white,
the human refuse of their manias and maladjustments.
These lost boys and the Black Panthers deserve the
name, and will acquire it, of the new Uncle Toms, the
caricatures of the Negro. Together they make the mere
blackness in certain circumstances a flag of danger to
white and black. This is simply a raw fact of life with
which one must deal. Some may even find that the in-
jection of danger into city life adds a flick of exhilara-
tion. (This would be taken as tactless or preferably
"racist.")

The grim joke on the North, both black and white,
is the constant arrival of Negro farmhands from the
South, their bus fare North often paid by the Southern
whites. These immediately go on welfare, and some
plunge into robbery, rape, and killing, first against
Northern Negroes, eventually against anybody. The
iron law of the ghetto is that the black criminal must
be protected by all blacks. This is enforced by terror,
including lye in the face. In consequence every ghetto's
ultimate rulers are the criminals. The decent majority
is helpless. The ghetto is far more dangerous than the
African jungle. (Blacks say all this, but don't like to
hear it from whites.)

The brave new word is "racism," which was not in
prewar dictionaries. Granted, one expects everybody to
be proud of his race, but this must mean too proud.

The companion word is "genocide," here meaning extermination of Negroes. But an inferior white teacher is said to commit "mental genocide" on black children. The paranoia implied by these words can inspire atrocious behavior, in a pattern common in insane asylums, where it justifies the paranoiac in expecting a terrible punishment. America of course is not an insane asylum. It is still a dream, and Negro success is now a part of that dream. (This is both too rough and too fancy.)

There are data to confirm the dream. In 1966, 23 per cent of nonwhite families had annual incomes of better than $7,000; outside the South the figure was 38 per cent. In the 1960s there was a 50 per cent rise of nonwhites in professional, technical, and managerial jobs, 48 per cent in clerical jobs, 32 per cent in selling jobs, and so on. Nearly 60 per cent of nonwhite adult males are now high school graduates, and about 10 per cent of Negro adult males are college graduates, thus closing in rapidly on the percentages for white adult males. In five years, Negroes in menial jobs have decreased by six hundred thousand while at the same time the total of employed Negroes has increased by about one million. This is a social miracle on an unprecedented scale. (Sounds harmless, but it leads to the following.)

The question nobody asks is: How much is enough? The opportunity for the qualified Negro is approaching equality; the problem now is to qualify the rest. In prep school and college admissions the unqualified Negro is favored over the qualified white. Backward white boys will soon be dyeing their skin dark. The United States at this moment spends over $15 billion a year on the colored minority. Is this enough, or too much?

Do we continue until the last Negro derelict has a station wagon and credit card? The real terror of Negro leaders is not genocide but this quiet question: How much is enough? (Obviously we have not gotten there yet.) This is why the crusade must invoke unreal issues such as three hundred years of degradation (compounded annually?), guilt for the ghetto, spiritual genocide, racism, revolution, the threat to "burn the cities," which will hold good to eternity. (This would please ungenerous whites, but horrify Negroes.)

Perhaps the elevation of a mass to equality is unprecedented because it is impossible. For there is no norm of equality. The rising man can be sure he is equal only when he is superior. Every stage of the process is invidious. The freed defendant is suddenly the judge. The patient becomes the doctor. The servant becomes the master. He must tell the majority, "If I am normal, you are clearly crazy." In the end the Negro will find that no two men are equal. (Imagine a politician saying any of this.)

Nor is Negro society geared to regenerative self-elevation. Successful Negroes in the white society (for that is what America is) are rejected by the ghettoes, and move out. The field is left to the militants, the new Uncle Toms, who want to be conspicuous and weave and bob and jump around to stay in the beam of the spotlight. These are the ones who see themselves as awesome national figures. But America is a large nation of about 180 million whites, most of whom rarely see a black face. As a face-to-face issue, the Negro is less of a problem than the gypsy moth. When these people see Negro insurrections on TV, they are likely to compare them to the "day in infamy": Pearl Harbor. (This would seem sheer rabble-rousing.)

Meanwhile, millions of individual Negroes have turned in a proud and brilliant performance in the American society. But one must see this at firsthand. Negro politicians never mention it, for to do so would be an admission of progress for the Negro. White politicians never mention it, for they want to take full credit to themselves for any Negro advance. The Black Panthers never mention it, because they consider the successful Negroes Uncle Toms. The white segregationists never mention it, because they can't bear the idea.

Whether the truth has been told here, and whether the politicians have told it, are left to the judgment of the reader.

For in November 1968, on this record, the harrowing question was whether the whites would vote for faith or fear, magnanimity or survival. The people as usual did their own research and thinking. The basic magnanimity of the American system and people struggled against group resentment and fear. Wallace—like Lenin in 1917 and Hitler in the Depression—the latest of the swindlers piping men down to despair and death, was sure the answer would be a vote for fear.

One virtue of the foregoing account is that it completely explains the 1968 election. The white South gave Wallace over 5 million votes and five states (Georgia, Alabama, Mississippi, Louisiana, Arkansas) and Nixon about 6 million votes and eight states. Add another 4 million Wallace votes in the North, and there is the ignominious fear-and-survival vote, about 15 million out of a total of over 70 million—not good, not bad.

The Humphrey vote of about 31 million was clearly for faith-and-magnanimity; and probably most of Nixon's Northern vote of about 25 million was Republican normality. The anti-Negro vote may have decided totals in such states as New Jersey, Ohio, and Illinois. Without the Negro issue, Humphrey would have won in a near-landslide. But Humphrey lost. The American Negro owes an unpaid and unacknowledged debt to the whites' cause of faith-and-magnanimity. Faith heavily outvoted fear; on balance white Americans voted their decency. (Imagine the reactions to the above of the Baldwins, Cleavers, Carmichaels; their foamings would be a death-cry, for these statements, if true, would revoke their vocation.)

Sensible black politicians must, and do, look at those 15 million committed adult anti-Negro votes, when there are only about 20 million Negroes in all. If the vast intelligent Negro majority cannot impose its will on the black society and the tiny cabal who are determined to debase the Negro aspiration, the anti-Negro vote will increase and harden. (A grim joke on the foamers but, worse, a grim joke on America.)

Here is a combustive political problem, and no politician has ever described it. The solution of course is below ideology and above politics; the word is decency. And the American people, perhaps alone in history, can afford to be decent.

The politicians cannot, though they probably know all this. When the people stop watching the politicians, as Hamlet said, "marry, this is miching mallecho, it means mischief."

The revolution in politics is the TV set. Now the

voters can look steadily at the faces of the candidates, sensing the composure, mania, smugness, fakery, candor, decency, energy, ruthlessness, greed, self-control, neurosis, in terms of the voter's lifetime experience of looking at people and checking their conduct against their appearance. I have faith in the people's intuitions when just looking, though a splendid mountebank may arrive to confound me.

Only look at him. When the words come out of him, speaking, he says, to "the issues," remember that the rules of the difficult game in a democracy compel him to ventilate only signals or clichés, not hard judgments on the true issues, the frightful problems of the people and the habitat. What he will say has virtually no significance beside what he is. As must have become apparent by now, he cannot tell you what he really thinks about anything. If in fact he can think.

The Negro situation in America today offered a convenient demonstration of this ingrown disability of the politician, but any other situation would serve the purpose, less flagrantly.

And thus to an apparent non sequitur. There is a gadget with which one can turn off the TV sound when the commercials come on. With this simple magic, the squealing, wheedling, bullying, infuriating salestalks, usually to music, always fortissimo, become an insane silent charade, inoffensive, impotent, and funny when the actors mouth and prance in involuntary dumb show. Suddenly the watcher's brain is not being manipulated; he is not the fool; instead the actors are the fools. It is that easy.

The same miracle can be applied to politics, and may

save the democratic system. Simply turn off the TV sound when the politician's face comes on the TV screen and look at him for a while without hearing his words. You won't be missing much, and you may learn everything.

❧ 14 ❧

The Africa Cliché

Any American of immigrant descent is axiomatically free to derive as much pride as he can from his overseas heritage. Much of the boasting along this line is ill-advised, starting with the Pilgrims. I have heard a Lithuanian-American base his pride on the claim that Lithuanians were members of the Order of Teutonic Knights. (They were, briefly, but the Order was founded to fight Lithuanians.) Rumanians call themselves the true descendants of the ancient Romans, meaning really Byzantines. Irishmen think Ireland was the most cultivated state in Europe in the sixth century. (There was not much competition.) Germans admire Hermann the War Man (Battle of Teutoburger Wald) and the Holy Roman Emperors. Englishmen think England has never been invaded since 1066. The two greatest races in the world, in their own opinion, are the French and Italians. And so on.

Negroes in their new status naturally and legitimately want to join the club of proud immigrants with a proud overseas history, the equal of, or preferably superior to, anybody else's history. Thus they must revert to the history of sub-Saharan Africa. And this is being done by patriotic black teachers to black children in the New York City schools, and elsewhere, with loving racist devotion and pride. A requisite here is an inquest into African history in search of an African Homer and Socrates and Alexander and Augustus and Charlemagne and Leonardo and Shakespeare to flesh out the epic glories of a vast and iridescent black racism, like a black pearl the size of a watermelon. Nothing less will do, for the black teachers must surpass the white racism they remember from the white South, the mad dream of a hallucinatory Confederacy. The fact that the children must survive in the non-racist North, whose ancestors destroyed that Confederacy, is of small account.

The black teacher, after a little research, has tidings of great joy. He can give the black children the glorious hypothesis that the first man appeared in East Africa, and may have been black, though of course skin color is not indicated by ancient bones. (A more likely theory is that the species first evolved east of the Caspian, in Asia.) He can also show the children reproductions of artifacts of the last few centuries produced by both Moslem and pagan African cultures, usually in West Africa, and acclaimed in the 1920s by such magazines as *Vanity Fair*. These are "interesting" but would not disturb Leonardo.

Soon the black teacher must begin to describe Africa. As for a day in the African tropics, there must be some good moments, if one is young and healthy, the bugs let up, and a breeze is blowing, perhaps a sense of physical license and even joy. From this, well-presented, a splendor of negritude may be adduced. The teacher must move on to specific facts of African life, and must arrive at a mystique based on cassava root, roast monkey, and the tsetse fly, a package very difficult to sell to any young American of any skin color. In some areas of Africa the rain comes down at well over a hundred inches a year, and steams in steady temperatures of well over 100° F., and favors a variety of endemic diseases, unfortunately without nearby medical clinics or welfare agencies. Class dismissed.

The black teacher can still find in African history Alexanders and Charlemagnes. There was the Zulus' King Chaka, who evolved the short-handled, long-bladed, stabbing assagai (word derived from the white North African Berbers). With his allied tribes, he swept all before him, a veritable Alexander. But he carried it too far. He wiped out all Negro life in an area about a thousand miles across, except his own tribes. His prototype is not Alexander, but Genghis Khan, or perhaps Hitler or Stalin. When the white Dutch arrived, fleeing the English, they were amazed to find the landscape absolutely empty until at last they approached the royal kraal of King Dingaans in Natal. The Zulu had depopulated Southeast Africa. The sophisticated word for this, about to become a cliché, is genocide.

Before the whites arrived, similar but less effective genocides were in course chiefly along the southern edge of the Sahara, from Senegal, Nigeria, Dahomey, to the Congo, Sudan, and Somaliland. The whites stopped the massacres and in some cases initiated much milder slaughters of their own, but these latter are now more famous than the far more terrible massacres that preceded them. The black genocides did not give the victims time to protest, or a medium to protest in. The black deaths did not produce an *Iliad* or *Song of Roland*. Without a literature, without elegies, death becomes nameless.

When Black Africa was freed and the whites departed, what happened? In due course the black genocide resumed, in full fury. At the moment the Moslem northern Nigerians are attempting to impose genocide on one of the most talented of Negro races, the Biafrans or Ibos, with the approval, at one time, of the whole organization of African states. This last fact by itself tells any sensible person all he needs to know about the morality and ultimate destiny of Black Africa. Another black genocide is taking place on the other side of Africa, in the southern Sudan, and others are imminent all over Africa. The peculiar mentalities of Stalin and Hitler would be perfectly understandable in Africa.

Now, what has all this horror to do with American Negroes?

Nothing. Exactly nothing. I would hope.

Most black Americans are removed from Africa by 150 to 300 years, longer than most white Americans are removed from Europe. Black Americans of today have no responsibility ("guilt") for anything that happens or has happened in Africa. The black racist teachers who hope to glorify black racism with Black African history are either ignorant, stupid, or debased. In the marvelous phrase freely used by black jokers against honorable whites, they are "racist monsters," and in this application the phrase is exactly descriptive, not a cliché. For the history must give the innocent children an instinct for genocide, the will to kill or die in large numbers. In the history, blacks typically kill blacks; the killing of whites is unusual, though it was achieved briefly by the Zulus, the Basutos (another talented African people), the black Moslem army of the Mahdi in the Sudan, the Ethiopians, and earlier in America by the Djukas and the Haitians.

The definitive question, which ends the nonsense, was asked a black militant on radio: "Would you now prefer that your ancestors had not been brought as slaves to America? That is, would you prefer to be a native African?" In all probability most Americans, black or white, would rather not run the risks of returning to their countries of origin. But one must suspect that nearly every American Negro is overjoyed not to be an African.

But the black jokers have another joke. Why not create Black Africa in the United States? Since blacks don't like snow, they would propose to pitch the black subcontinent in Alabama, Mississippi, perhaps Louisiana, South Carolina, Georgia, their 10-per-cent share of the fifty American states. (They seem to have given up on the resort state of Florida, which would connect them with the black-populated Antilles.) To take this suggestion as if seriously, it would require all whites to move out of those states, with federal indemnities, but also all Negroes, of whatever status or shade of skin color, to be transported compulsorily into those states, leaving the other forty-five states lily-white except for a few Indians and Orientals. Anybody can develop the farce from there. All Negro athletes would be stripped from the teams of the forty-five states, and all Negro entertainers from their theater, movies, TV, and radio.

White-owned industry would stay for a while, until expropriated, to take advantage of the cheap labor. The United States Navy would convoy ships down the Mississippi. Florida, with its space program, would become a large Guantanamo. Alabama might even develop the assagai and depopulate Mississippi. The Atlanta baseball team, if its white owners were not expelled, would win the World Series every year. In fact, if the intelligent Negroes could keep control (doubtful), Black America might become a wonder of the world.

Some Northern whites might have no strong objection to giving the blacks at least Mississippi and Alabama, but the whites in residence there have some rights and some voice and some guns. Black America is of course a chimera, but the black jokers say they will launch guerrilla warfare to make it reality.

A grimmer joke can hardly have been invented in the whole history of the world, but it is essential to remember that it would remain a joke. The unfunny part of it is that in the course of the killings, democracy too would probably be a casualty. Once again it is all based on a cliché now repeated in the respectable white American and foreign press and sanctified as truth: that the very presence of Negroes in the United States is a despicable outrage, as if these people had just been dragged off slave ships in manacles and stood up on the auctioneer's block. But these pitiable chattels are driving Cadillacs and eating better than I do and damned glad this is their country.

Still, they fantasy the abominable humiliation in some other century. And for this they hold the recent white immigrations of Irish, Jews, Italians, Poles, and so on irremediably guilty. Hallucination upon hallucination, the black jokers weep; they cleverly watch themselves crying inside, hear the authentic gasp, and convince themselves that they are in a passion, as if ready to die. It is an actor's heroism, but this actor may actually die on stage. For such antics have always attracted the attention of Mr. Death, and suddenly He is there, looking in the window.

The black joke of Beautiful Africa invites the counter-joke of free passage for American blacks to Africa. But I cannot join in any such cleverness. If the story of Black Africa teaches a sense of the tragedy of blackness and a genetic self-pity, it is not fit for Americans.

The great mass of the Negro community instinctively rejects this history. The children may listen at first wide-eyed and credulous but they will eventually discover for themselves the monotony of Black African death, the black slave-traders who sold the blacks and are still in business today, the inglorious tale of Man in Black Africa, the monstrous inhumanity, and will look twice or three times at their loving black racist teachers.

Blackness in the Northern United States for the last hundred years has been disadvantaged, humiliated, unequal in opportunity, outside the society, but nothing that could be called tragic in historical terms, for such minorities have existed everywhere, and they still exist. These disabilities have been removed in the North, and to some extent even in the South. American blacks have no need to identify themselves with the tragedies of Black Africa, except in magnanimous sympathy, as some whites do.

The black American's pride and mystique will be more soundly founded on the talent, charm, energy, courage, culture, and good will of Black America.

Nobody asked me, but that's my opinion.

❧ 15 ❧

The Legal Cliché

"This is a government of laws, not of men," we hear now and then and, thinking of lynch law, we hastily agree. But of course it is only a cliché. It cannot be true, as long as we have the altogether admirable jury system. The fact is that this is, thank God, a government of laws *and* men. The cliché has not yet overwhelmed us.

Another cliché of the law is "innocent until proved guilty." Originally it was a magnificent protection of the accused. But to the grand principle has been added something often unnoticed, and it has been fossilized into a cliché that excludes much reality.

Millions watching on TV saw the reality of Jack Ruby killing Lee Harvey Oswald in a crowded room. Sirhan Sirhan's shooting of Robert F. Kennedy was also in a crowded room, and millions saw Sirhan being wrestled down, still clutching the gun. Subsequently, news an-

nouncers scrupulously called Sirhan "the alleged assassin" or "a suspect." The explanation for this Kafka
madness was that they did not want to "prejudice a fair
trial," for Sirhan and Ruby were still—haha—innocent
until proved guilty. But must a witness to a murder call
the murderer "alleged"? To the witnesses, murderers
are no longer "innocent until proved guilty"; they are
guilty, at the instant of the crime. The book is closed
for all the witnesses. The "due process" (both terms
have numerous definitions, giving a large product of
possible meanings) has become an empty formality.

The joke is that lawyers have decided that the only
people who can decide guilt are lawyers, conducting an
adversary trial before another lawyer called a judge.
The witnesses, even if they come in the millions, are
merely witnesses. Their opinion is only an opinion until the whole hierarchy of lawyers has drawn out to
the end its tralatitious charade. Meanwhile, all the witnesses watch this nonsense impatiently. And at long
last it turns out that the bloody hand is guilty, or perhaps it is not guilty.

Another cliché is that the same situations under law
must always produce the same verdict. Thus we have:
(1a) a man speeding his car; (1b) a man speeding his
car with his wife in advanced labor in the back seat;
(2a) a stranger paying in a restaurant with a bad check;
(2b) a man who has spent $35,000 in seven years in
the restaurant paying with a bad check; (3a) a man
killing a stranger; (3b) a boy disarming and killing a
stranger who has just killed the boy's father. Under our
legal system (2b) and (3b) were penalized as if they
had been (2a) and (3a). The case of (1b) is usually
handled by a policeman, who sensibly escorts the man

and wife to the hospital. In a "government of laws, not of men," the lawyer is obviously forbidden to use the good sense God gave him, and in this isolation from the living society, he is perfectly protected, coddled, and enriched.

Ideally, and the United States began with the grace of a nearly ideal Constitution, the Congress need rarely pass a new law except to adapt the society to a new situation; surely all necessary laws must have been enacted by preceding Congresses. Under such a naïve and annihilating eye, the record of the Congresses is interesting.

The Congresses and the state legislatures enact great windrifts of new laws, not for the people, the society, you and me, not even attempting to understand what may be the flaws in the going system, but primarily to satisfy various interested groups. These sterile but profitable (to somebody) statutes, having "lost precise meaning," if they ever had it, are clichés by the definition. They become stereotypes that are applied by law to all compatible situations.

One begins to suspect that our rulers do not know why we put them there. The first duty of a society, indeed the primary reason for a government, is not to rule its people but to protect them. Among other things, it must protect them from false accusation, as the Supreme Court has so nobly insisted. Very good. But some way ahead of this obligation of government is its duty to protect its people from being murdered by one another.

A murder is committed. The lawyer mentality sees that the murderee is dead and has no value; the murderer is alive. One can identify with the live murderer, but not with the dead murderee, and so the problem becomes how to salvage the murderer, since the murderee is beyond recall. The murderer, it is implied, is just like the rest of us except for this lamentable indiscretion of murder. Thus, a kindly assumption might describe the whole innocent population as potential murderers. Ostensibly gracious and noble, this assumption sweeps aside a very ancient and sacred law of man: remember and honor your dead. It further rips at the body of the people's loyalty to the government that makes this scandalous assumption.

For although the murderee is dead, some very important people survive: relatives, friends, and all the innocent bystanders, that is, the whole society. When they see that the murderer is not punished, they realize insensibly that the murderee had no value, and that they too in this society have no value.

Actually, the disposal of the murderer is not important beside the relationship of all these people to the society. Public policy requires their loyalty; it can utterly dispense with the murderer. In a moral and a civic sense, he has virtually ceased to exist. An increase in so-called capital punishment might not decrease crime—that would not be its purpose—but it would immediately heighten the citizen's sense of being protected by his society and his sense of his own value. These are extremely important considerations for a government that wishes to survive. It is not sufficiently understood, especially by our rulers, that when a crime is committed the true defendant, and the true victim, is the state. The question then becomes, Which is to survive: the criminal or the state?

The alternative to a permissive state, sweetly indulgent of crime against itself and its people, is the Mafia, which is flourishing. Somewhat similar protection is extended by such other groups as police, newspapermen, Negroes, and some labor unions. Whether good or bad, this is part of the social process.

Should the citizen finally decide that he can preserve his own value only by killing his devaluer, that is, his prospective murderer, society will have taken one step too many into the kindly permissive morality. The next step might be the *condottieri*, such as the Malatesta of Rimini, men who measure their value in violence. And has not the society approached self-satire when the word permissiveness is easily extended to murder? Some horrid laughter is permissible, if one is cynical and not especially averse to dying, or if one is a murderer.

A valid criticism of the law is that there is a remote and delayed connection between social process and legal process. For example, Negroes move increasingly into responsible jobs in the white society, where they had never been before. This is social process. At this point they are exactly equal, under the law, to their white co-workers. But in fact it turns out that some of these Negroes import, not unnaturally, some of the manners and patterns of the murderous ghetto into the generalized society. A black girl in an office snarls at a white girl, "I'll get you." The white girl barks back, "Are you threatening me?" The black girl mumbles. Later, leaving the office, the white girl is mugged by two blacks. Here too we see, in its classic form, the social process. The law is ethereally above all these agonizing and well-understood social processes, until much, much later, when an adversary case reaches a trial court, goes to an appellate court, and perhaps at last to the Supreme Court, where the legal process tries to grip the social process with its attenuated and unwieldy tongs. But by then the social process has proceeded still further.

Given the unpredictable dynamism of social life, some part of this failure is inevitable and forgivable. But lawyers, including judges, read little or no general, humanistic, or philosophical literature, and hence see the social process only when it comes to them as an adversary case. Their professional training, to the limit of its powers, painstakingly cripples their native ability to think humanly and realistically on the subject. And very few of them, as of any other specialized group, are capable of any original thinking or of putting it down on paper as writing.

And yet this lamed group runs the United States. Of the United States Congress, about 60 per cent are always lawyers, in the Senate alone about 68 per cent. A recent count of state governors showed 66 per cent were lawyers. State legislatures, regulatory agencies, and so on carry the same or higher percentages of lawyers. Iowa's congressmen from 1844 to 1938 were 76 per cent lawyers, 309 out of 419. In 1835 de Tocqueville identified the lawyers as the only American aristocracy he could discern.

One must begin to wonder whether this congestion of lawyers in government may be inevitable, whether lawyers alone know how to govern. (The answer is No.) A recent English Parliament had, in a total of 630 members, 116 businessmen, 105 workers, 47 journalists and writers, 35 farmers, and only 129 lawyers, or about 20 per cent of the Parliament. A healthy, balanced legislature would seem to be possible and work-able, without the domineering fetishes and vices of the legal mind. Research on the constituents of other parliaments would undoubtedly show something nearer the British than the American proportion.

Active lawyers in the United States today total three hundred thousand (forty thousand of them in government), as against only thirty thousand British lawyers. The American lawyers' median income is $13,000, and in 1966 legal services cost America $4 billion.

These last figures come from Martin Mayer's amazingly comprehensive *The Lawyers*, which for all its virtues fails to crystallize the apparently uncrystallizable subject of law in America. The book does not at all suggest, as I have, that the vice in American law is too many lawyers, but it graphs the plurality of lawmaking factories, which make jobs and more work for lawyers.

The untalented legislatures (in popular opinion, not their own) conceive, write, and enact new laws. The trial courts try to apply them. The appellate courts try to relate them to previously written and appealed law. The Supreme Court tries to settle the confusion, and sometimes compounds it. The legislatures may then pass new laws to frustrate the interpretations of the courts.

Operative law, in the handling of the accused, is meanwhile made by the police and the district attorneys.

The law digests, reviews, and reports make still more operative law, since, for example, most lawyers read only the digests' headnotes on current appellate cases. The cumulative law literature is enough to break the head of any lawyer or judge who tries to read it all.

Unknown to the layman, the lawyer's education is fatally tralatitious.

Still more operative law is made by the regulatory agencies (FCC, FPC, SEC, ICC, etc.), which make their own rules. There is also the totalitarian Internal Revenue Service, which makes its own law, submitted to three different lines of courts, all of whom the IRS ignores, and just keeps on litigating until it wins in some court. There are also the labor union negotiation lawyers who make law that affects the whole society, often disastrously.

This is a crude summary of American law as it bears on every citizen of the republic, directly or indirectly. As so defined, it is a travesty of any concept whatsoever of law and order. The true subversive in America, it would thus appear, is the American lawyer and judge, granted his good and even high intentions, even when he is an official of government, or rather especially so.

United States reference law books each year report thirty thousand appellate decisions; the British system reports only three hundred. In addition, the bedlam of government agency decisions is described by various looseleaf services. One figure for United States federal, state, and local laws is 1,156,644 laws. One needs no more than this fantastic number to see the law as the gibbering climax of an old mania.

Mayer's remarkable survey reveals a more profound pathology of the American legal system. The court is "irrevocably neutral," even when right and wrong are obvious; there are no blacks and whites, only shades of gray. In liability cases the courts ignore the fact that the real defendant is the insurance company. The courts are concerned not with public policy but only with law and lawyers; they are wholly outside the society. "Large areas of the law are an incoherent mess." Many laws are meaningless or have "any number of meanings," offering an open field to lawyers and judges. Commonly, legislatures pass laws whose possible applications they have hardly considered. Some of the scandalous federal laws are Robinson-Patman (fully dismembered in Adelman's *A & P: A Study in Price-Cost Behavior and Public Policy*), Clayton, and the Trade Commission Act. "The incompetence of the law" is a common and acceptable expression. Congress simply ignores the complex problem of the regulatory agencies, which wield enormous power in the whole society. So bad is the judiciary that the New York Legal Aid Society won reversals on 55 per cent of its cases before 1965.

We have still further cause to wonder about American law. American penalties for crimes are four to ten times more severe than those of any other civilized nation. Internal Revenue regulations are impenetrably complex. The cruelties of the various bureaucracies are in their way as arbitrary as the cruelties of the feudal system. Labor union negotiations are wholly outside the law; the talent required of labor lawyers is that of screaming and taking insults. The routine procedure of reducing the charge in exchange for a plea of guilty to a lesser charge is entirely illegal.

An egregious example of corrupt law was the Supreme Court's decision that the publisher of *Eros* magazine was a wicked man because some subordinate had promoted the magazine under the postmark of the Pennsylvania towns of Intercourse and Blue Ball, not at all because the published magazine was wicked. The obvious thought is that these towns are actual towns, and that their founding fathers, in naming them, were not making obscene or frivolous jokes. To misread the meaning of the towns' founders must reveal a leaning toward obscenity, and in this case in the Supreme Court. And so the Supreme Court shamed itself. The self-respecting and honorable towns of Intercourse and Blue Ball remain, while the Supreme Court trespasses into value judgments on manners, an area in which it has never been assigned jurisdiction.

More can be said. The need for reapportionment of Congressional districts was flagrantly obvious, and so this Court made it difficult. The elaboration of dissenting opinions is a remarkably futile form of judicial introspection. The ordering of new trials by superior courts looks to many critics like double jeopardy. The adversary and appeal system of procedure is the worst possible way to find, collate, and present the truth of any situation. Most people have come to recognize the law as the deadly enemy of justice.

The myth of American jurisprudence is that the lawyers and the courts are building a mighty cathedral for the centuries. On a closer look, we see that they are busy on a claptrap, collapsing scaffolding around the splendid Constitution of the United States. These people may have debased even the Constitution to a cliché, may God have mercy on their souls.

⤳§ 16 §⤲

Metaphor and Simile Clichés

There must be thousands of subgroups of Americans who have evolved localized vocabularies of clichés. This might be a suitable field for graduate students, but not for the present writer. What are given here are some standard American metaphors and similes whose literal meaning has been almost entirely forgotten and is not typically envisaged by the user.

There is no intent to invade the vast field of American slang. In fact, hardly one-sixth of the expressions given are included in *Dictionary of American Slang* by Wentworth and Flexner, a conscientious work running to 655 pages. Metaphor, its preface points out, occurs in slang as anywhere else, but it is not essential to slang. The suggestive fact is that in reading these dictionaries of slang, one has a sense of compulsive stupidity, of degradation and oppression, of discouragement about the human kind. Slang pitilessly exposes the human brain as something one would prefer not to acknowledge. There are, for example, about 320 slang synonyms for intoxicated.

Metaphors and similes, on the contrary, are lively, naïve, and, in general, no discredit to the race. Those that follow are familiar to most people and do not define any particular subgroup.

ABSOLUTE DETERRENCE. Lower the boom.

AMBITIOUS. Eager beaver, on the make, empire builder.

AMERICA. Peanut butter.

ASTOUND. Rock back on his heels, stand on his ear.

BACK DOWN. Eat crow.

BEDRAGGLED. Something the cat dragged in, drowned rat, dog, shark bait.

BLIND. As a bat, mole.

BOLD. As brass (brazen).

BRIGHT. As a penny, button.

BUSY. As a beaver, bee, bedbug, bird dog, one-armed paperhanger. Up to the neck.

CHARMS. The birds off the trees.

CHIVALRY. White Southerners.

CLEAN. As a whistle, hound's tooth.

COLD. As ice, a cucumber, she mouse's belly, a witch's teat.

CONCEITED. Too big for his breeches, hinkty (Negro), stuck up.

COULDN'T HIT. A barn door, broad side of a barn, bull's backside with a bull fiddle.

CRANKY. Got out the wrong side of the bed.

CRAZY. As a loon, coon, coot, bedbug, jaybird. Off his rocker, trolley. Mad as a hatter. Nutty as a fruit-cake. Lost his marbles.

CRAZY (*not*). Like a fox.

CRITIC. Hatchet man.

CROOKED. As a ram's horn, dog's hind leg, snake.

CRUCIAL FACTOR. The name of the game.

CUTE. As a button, bug's ear, kitten, little red wagon.

DEAD. As a doornail, dodo.

DEFERRED ACCEPTANCE. Give me a rain check.

DETERMINATION. Till hell freezes over, I'm blue in the face.

DISASTROUS DENOUEMENT. The wheels came off, fat's in the fire, cat's in the dovecote, fox in the hencoop. All hell broke loose.

DOG (*country*). Ugly brute.

DOG (*city*). Mummy's little angel.

DRUNK. As a lord, skunk. Three sheets to the wind. Lit up like a Christmas tree. Boiled: owl. High: kite. Tight: tick.

DULL (*two senses*). As ditchwater. Won't cut warm butter.

DUMB. As an ox, dodo, plumber's helper, fence post.

EASY. As pie, falling off a log, taking candy from a baby. Snap. Lead-pipe cinch.

ELECTRONICALLY EAVESDROPPED. Bugged.

EXASPERATED. Bugged.

FAILURE. Flop, turkey, bomb. Laid an egg.

FAST-BALL PITCHER. Flamethrower.

FREE. As a bird, breeze, air.

FRESH (*two senses*). As a daisy, newmown hay; spit, paint.

FRIVOLITY (*not all*). Gas and gaiters, beer and skittles.

GENTLE. As a lamb.

GOING. Like the proverbial hotcakes.

GREAT INVENTION. Tin can.

GREEDY. As a pig, on the take.

GUEST. Freeloader.

HAPPY. As a lark, clam, bedbug.

HARD. As nails, rock.

HARASSED. Cat on a hot tin roof.

HOMELY. As sin, a hedge fence.

HOPELESS. Not a Chinaman's chance.

HOT (*several senses*). As a pistol, biscuit, hell, Tophet, $2 pistol.

HUNGRY. As a bear, wolf.

INACCESSIBLE. "He just stepped away from his desk."

INFORMATION (*good*). From the horse's mouth.

INORDINATE. Out of line.

INSCRUTABLE. Clam, sphinx, Chinese pagoda.

LAZY. As a hound dog.

LITTLE OR NOTHING. Drop in the bucket.

LUCK. Of the Irish.

MAD. As a wet hen. Fumious.

MERRY. As a grig.

MIND. Like a steel trap, wizard.

MISCEGENATION (*polite form*). Integration.

MISDIRECTED EFFORT. Bull in a china shop.

NARCISSIST. Swinger.

NEAT. As a pin.

NEEDED (*not*). Like a hole in the head.

NEUROSIS. Hangup.

NOT LIKELY. Hopefully.

OBSOLETE. Horse and buggy, senior citizen.

OLD. As Methuselah. Older than God.

OVERWHELM. Eat for breakfast.

PHONY. As a $3 bill.

PLAIN (*three senses*). As a mud fence, old shoe, pikestaff.

PRETTY. As a picture, paint.

PROBABILITY OF FIRE. Smoke.

PROBLEM. Hot potato.

PROMISING PARVENU. Diamond in the rough.

PROUD. As a peacock, Punch.

RAGE. Climb the walls, hit the ceiling, chew the carpet, blow one's top, fly off the handle, fit to be tied, do a slow burn.

RAPID. Bat out of hell, blue streak, like sixty.

REACTION. Backlash, backfire.

RED. As a beet.

REPETITIVENESS. Phonograph record.

RICH. As Croesus. Filthy.

RISKY. On thin ice.

RISKY INVESTMENT. A pig in a poke.

SHARP. As a nail, knife, razor, tack.

SILENCE. You could have heard a pin drop.

SINISTER. Smiler with a knife.

SLEEP. Like a top, log, baby, rock.

SLOW. As a snail, molasses in January.

SMART. As a whip, paint.

SMOOTH. As a baby's behind, silk.

SNUG. As a bug in a rug.

SOCIALISM. Pie in the sky.

STANDS OUT. Like a sore thumb, skunk in a fog, good deed in a naughty world.

STATES' RIGHTS. "Dixie," the Confederate flag, the United States Senate.

STIFF. As a ramrod, pike, board.

STRONG. As a bull, ox, horse.

SURPRISE ARRIVAL. "I'd have baked a cake."

SWEAR. Like a trooper.

SUCCESSFUL AT THE MOMENT. Hot as a pistol, ball of fire, high on the hog, got it made, riding high.

SWEET. As pie, sugar.

TOUGH. As shoeleather.

UGLY. As sin, mud fence. Would stop a clock.

VIRTUE. All sweetness and light.

WRONG. Shoe on the wrong foot, booboo, all wet.

Fortunately, the reader understands all these clichés but for posterity or translation into another language they would all need precise definition, which will not be given here. For example, under rage, an extreme but fairly harmless tantrum is conveyed by climb the walls, chew the carpet; fly off the handle and blow one's top are the active tantrums, usually ill-advised; hit the ceiling is authoritarian; fit to be tied may be explosive but is still inactive; do a slow burn is repressed resentment that will probably not explode; and mad as a wet hen suggests flustered, impotent anger which may, like some of the others, amuse the bystanders. In the expressions, we can deduce that the bystanders are generally unimpressed by the rage.

The rural origin of these metaphors and similes is obvious. The recurrence of bedbug and paint is interesting, expressing a transition from filth to cleanliness in the nineteenth century, perhaps. The violence attributed to the American by the new critics may seem confirmed, but I think a better word would be wildness, partly inherited from the Anglo-Saxon style. As can be seen, it is actually a pretense of violence, or bluff, a crude form of manners, which everybody understands and enjoys except the new critics.

Since such clichés are the hardest working machinery in the American language, it is pointless to say they sound childish. Actually, if we heard a child using them, we would be repelled by his precocity. Such a child would have a false maturity which might well cripple for life his ability to find the reality for himself, behind the metaphor. One usually encounters such children only in backward communities or in the South.

The acknowledged American master of the cliché, S. J. Perelman, invokes very different clichés for a much more specialized audience. He may use such terms as: rank flattery, schoolboy crush, puppy love, snail's pace, but these mild clichés are not yet perfectly fossilized; some residue of the metaphor is still alive. With the kind of clichés listed above, he does not find it necessary to spell them out, thus, "his story a tissue." He shops for his clichés all over the English-speaking world; one would like to see his version of a *Finnegans Wake*. Thus: fun-loving American boy who likes to fish with a bent pin. Lick his weight in wildcats. Law of the jungle, dog eat dog, root or die. The saxophones start sobbing. Saucy-eyed. The only game in town. Sticky wicket. Brimful of euphoria. At concert pitch. Quidnunc. He struck me on the bugle and drew claret. In full fig. Quandary. Teak-paneled walls. A blintz fit for a prince. Freeze my blood. Polo coat draped over his shoulders.

Perelman rarely stoops to being directly witty: Harry Hypotenuse, the sum of the squares. Perelman scavenges the overstated and the smug. But he is in fact echoing, with a leer, a whole spectrum of life styles, and less enlightened readers cannot possibly identify the echoes. A man who normally uses "all wet" would not know how to read "brimful of euphoria" or "saxophones start sobbing" and would take "lick his weight

in wildcats" or "dog eat dog" straight. Perelman's people are delicately pretentious; they think they are
"where it's happening." His ear is so fine that he catches
terms that have been used only once or twice too often,
such as "root or die," "at concert pitch," or "quidnunc."
Kahn and Fiedler should be ripe vineyards for Perelman.

Now, to revert to the first chapter, consider translat-
ing the list of metaphor-similes into French in the year
2070. Some are so blatant that they would be compre-
hensible in any time or tongue. Others would be quite
mystifying. "Happy as a clam" is an example of the
former; "lower the boom" and "eat for breakfast" are
probably examples of the latter.

Perelman's interstitial clichés, on the other hand,
would probably translate almost literally, but not as
clichés. For the echoes would long since have vanished.
The translator would have real trouble with "his story a
tissue" and "the sum of the squares." The reader would
be baffled by "polo coat draped over his shoulders," and
other life styles of the period that Perelman has noticed.
For Perelman (as well as Kahn and Fiedler) is in the
business of expressing the inexpressible. And as a rule
the inexpressible is not exactly true. The man with a
coat slung over his shoulders is not necessarily, as is
implied, a complete phony. The man might be George
Washington or Walt Whitman or James Joyce.

❧ 17 ❧

The Vital Cliché

On such a subject as this, the reader is fully as qualified
an authority as the writer. And so it is left to him to
finish this book. Pages 179–184 have been supplied to
permit him to fill in any of the harmless metaphor-
simile clichés he finds, the pitiful jargon clichés, the
snobbish life-style clichés. Several further pages are
assigned to the vital idea clichés. These are often vague
concepts that are never expressed but decisively condition the individual's opinions and behavior. An example is the slang word, "jerk," or "creep." Some time
ago any young person felt competent to identify a jerk
and had no misgivings about his judgment. With the
passage of time he discovered that some of these identi-
fiable jerks became people of distinction, power, or
wealth. He thus lost some confidence in his judgment.
In the end one is left with a choice among three clichés:
(1) there are still jerks; (2) nobody is a jerk; (3) every-

body is a jerk. In the writer's opinion, none of these choices is better than the others. But the reader's judgment will be strongly affected by the one he has chosen. Here he can write it down, think it over and, if he likes, debate it with his friends. He may even organize a chapter of Clichés Anonymous, and move the whole subject into Group Therapy. For it is the peculiar charm and power of clichés that they are anonymous.

It is to be hoped that the reader has not concluded that this subject is a tissue of small jokes. In such a cliché as "You can't trust anyone over thirty," or "Anyone who disagrees with me is crazy," we see the attempt to dissolve this society. It will therefore be instructive to list some opposing clichés.

The warning must be given that this routine procedure will be torture for the juvenile, doctrinaire, or credulous.

Science will eventually discover the last secret of the universe.	Man will never wholly understand this universe.
Nature is crude and inefficient.	Nature is magnificent.
Man is this planet's masterpiece.	Man is this planet's great vermin.
Play is man's highest function.	Work is man's highest function.
Unions are the new aristocracy.	Unions are hungry.
One should love the whole world.	One should love one's own habitat.
Dislike of America is chic.	Treason is not yet a nice word.

The expatriate is chic.

Remember Napoleon, Stalin, Hitler?

American society is still Puritan.

America is everything, all at once.

Loneliness is the great disease.

It's wonderful to be alone.

Sensitivity is the prime virtue.

Fortitude is the prime virtue.

Having is good.

Doing without is good.

Atomic war is unthinkable.

Better think about it.

Life must give one a reason for existence.

Gee, it's great to be alive.

Most of the truth is already in print.

Very little truth is in print.

Any nation's population must increase.

This earth cannot take any more population.

Present affluence must go on forever.

The "crash" is due in fifty years.

Unselfish patriotism is for fools.

Patriotism is a debt to posterity.

Elite is an obsolete word.

Without elites, no society at all.

Mountaineering is heroic.

It is only a test of seriousness.

California is sanctuary for the old.

California is earthquake country.

Any starvation is a disgrace to civilization.

Overpopulation is a prior disgrace to civilization.

Negroes are the same as whites.

Negroes are different, maybe superior.

Power must be abolished.

Power is eternal.

Communists really love mankind.

Communists have plans for mankind.

Blackmail occurs only in fiction.

Half the male population are blackmailable.

Sacco and Vanzetti were innocent.

Flatfootedly guilty.

Government agencies take good care of our national resources.

They are their worst enemies.

Highways are the No. 1 priority.

We have too many highways.

A nation can be invented.

A nation is a biological growth that cannot be faked.

Any new nation is wonderful.

New nations are latent disasters.

The young ought to know sex biology.

Sex is a strictly amateur art.

The telephone is indispensable.

AT & T may be the most irresponsible and greedy U.S. monopoly.

A convicted criminal is sorry.

He profoundly admires his crime.

The citizen's duty is only to call police.

Public order is the business of all citizens.

The private eye is fictional.

U.S. private police outnumber public police.

Farce is harmless fun.

Farce leads to revolution.

Moral judgments are easy.

Morality leads to exaggeration.

Males are superior to females.

The separate male was a fairly late invention of nature's (11th phylum of 13 phyla).

The cliché can certainly be identified as one of the most powerful phenomena in human social life. It should be the subject of intense inquiry by the social scientists, though I do not think they have yet noticed it. In any such study it would become apparent that anything that is easily available, even if it is perfection or happiness, soon becomes boring to this species, man. Crazy as this statement sounds, if it is referred to anybody's past life it will be recognized after due thought as historical. The perfections and happiness of the past have gone.

One can go back beyond the individual's past. The Greeks of the age of Praxiteles perfected sculpture (and probably also painting). Their successors, taught by the masters, probably could have repeated the perfection but disdained a duplication that would have won them no reputation. There followed the sentimentality, histrionic realism, and gigantism of the Hellenistic Age.

The Renaissance perfectly mastered painting. Bored with this perfection, the eighteenth- and nineteenth-century painters explored sentimentality, the histrionic, the satirical, but still knew what they were doing. The essential pose of Impressionism was that the painter, even Renoir, was not trying very hard. The later painters veered into every sort of aberration, each to be repudiated by the next and wilder aberration. The painters, and also the customers, were bored by the old perfections, which had become clichés, by Delacroix, Corot, Goya, Daumier. Numbers of untalented painters appeared who could paint successful forgeries of the old masters. The majestic secrets were no longer secrets; they were the common coin of any art school.

But nobody wants to be the new Rembrandt; he wants to be the first, only, and original Jack Sprat.

No statement can say everything. All the things it omits struggle to get said too, and this struggle takes the form of turning the original statement into a cliché and killing it. The British Empire was a splendid statement, but it overlooked a good deal, such as the latent talents of the "natives." The virtues of the Empire can still be argued; Winston Churchill believed in it to the end, but he too was too verbal about his imperialism. The Empire was becoming a cliché. The memory of Agincourt had become a phonograph record of an actor's imitation of Shakespeare's Henry V:

> . . . and gentlemen in England now abed
> Shall think themselves accursed they were not here,
> And hold their manhoods cheap whiles any speaks
> That fought with us upon Saint Crispin's Day,

this last with a towering shout that certainly was not given on the great field, but today moves and entertains Americans. The cliché is thus completed, instead of remaining an unspoken mystery inside the head of an English patriot who would gladly have died for it.

The best insurance for an idea against the fate of becoming a cliché is to remain unspoken or, better, unspeakable, as was the word for God among the Biblical Hebrews. The second best is to become the exclusive monopoly of an elite or priesthood, as the secrets of religion and medicine were held by the ancient Egyptian priesthood. But an idea open to exact examination, at first admiringly, then routinely, then critically, as in the modern free world, is mortal.

Sometimes powerful ideas invent their own destructive satires. Thus, the Manchu Empire had the Dowager Empress; the Czarist Empire, Rasputin; Napoleon, the Hundred Days; the French Army, the Dreyfus Case; the Ottoman Empire, the eunuchs. The Austrian Empire may have been ruined by waltzes and "The Merry Widow," and the American Confederacy by "Dixie." The difficulty of turning "The Star-Spangled Banner" into a cliché is that it is a fairly artless and unpretentious description of an event and rather difficult to sing. Its replacement by a more stirring anthem would be a grave mistake.

A curious footnote to this process is that the cliché of revolutionary France was expressed by a Corsican, that of Communist Russia by a Georgian, that of Nazi Germany by an Austrian. (The Nazi leadership was larded with Auslanders.) The outsider typically sees the cliché in a magnified form. In the Northern Hemisphere the cliché seems to ripen southward. Now the Negro movement in the United States shows the same symptom in finding many of its leaders from the West Indies, even as Napoleon's first wife came from Martinique.

The timely cliché in the form of such enormous lies as "land for everybody" or "the master race" makes a terrible impact on human history, and can survive for a while if the regime makes precise examination impossible or unspeakable, as was done in Nazi Germany and Communist Russia, and is now being attempted by the Negro militants against the black community. It often works. The result is a balance between terror and courage. Absolute terror negates courage. Absolute courage has sometimes dismayed the terror.

The cliché is the false courage of such groups as the

Black Panthers. The brave men are such as Doctor Martin Luther King, Jr., and others who turn their backs on the black terror, the most courageous men in America, black or white. The Black Panther, on the contrary, is a walking cliché, or joke, or enormity. In the new permissiveness, a murderous joke is evidently still a joke. But a cliché is doomed.

The mass media dramatize such jokes, inspiring in the mindless the eternal cliché, "Oh, that's where it's happening." For any individual the only place anything is "happening" is inside his own head, and nowhere else. The parvenu expression, for such it is even in the most *avant-garde* circles, used to be "keeping up with the Joneses." On this silly challenge, many people entirely lose their nerve. When they think nothing much is happening inside their heads, they cry "Oh, where is it happening?" Losing their nerve is perhaps the best thing they do. The last Czar of All the Russias died asking "Where is it happening?" Lenin might possibly have told him that where it was happening was the United States. Trotsky could have told Lenin.

At that time the actual power of the United States was veiled and thus could not have become a cliché. Since then it has been thoroughly understood, rationalized, evaluated, discredited, and translated, as has been shown in these pages, into various clichés. No further vituperation is needed. For America continues to escape the cliché formulations simply by being 200 million sovereign individuals, the document of the Constitution supported by the Declaration, and a complex of unspoken beliefs and faiths in the minds of the people, and all of these are quite beyond the comprehension of the cliché-makers.

In a free society the cliché-maker is allowed to aspire greatly, as to fossilize and obsolesce such diverse ideas as love, mother-love, love of the habitat (patriotism), loyalty, courage, the family, the moon, sex, a man, a woman, honor, peace, war, God, oxygen, photosynthesis, the universe. After all his operations, the undiminished and eternal reality of these phenomena still outstares the little poseur with his trickery of words. For some ideas are too indefinable, too diverse, too basic, too necessary to life, too spectral, too grossly human, to submit to the constriction of the cliché. Certainly a lot of cute little ideas come up in every generation and die, and at the moment the airs are throbbing with these desperate ephemera, poor things not destined even to become clichés outside tiny groups who know these passwords into oblivion. But who am I to know? In fact, I do not know.

New ideas are not brought to birth or death so quickly in other societies. In a free, open, dynamic world such as America the turnover of ideas is very rapid, and the mortality is probably close to 99 per cent. In Eastern Europe and most of Asia, new ideas of whatever merit appear with much more difficulty and, if they survive at all, last much longer. The habit of thinking in the same old way is characteristic of Russia, Czarist or Communist, in the fashion once called Byzantine, for Moscow once claimed to be the new Byzantium, "the Third Rome," a marvelous boast no longer heard, for the two-thousand-year-old cliché of Caesar is no longer named Czar. But the cliché survives, as do clichés generally in Russia, with ferocious tenacity. The observation leads, incidentally, to serious doubt whether Russian Communism will be liberalized in the near future. Accepting the cliché signal, it is more likely, more Russian, that another Stalin, or Ivan the Terrible, will take over the Kremlin.

It may be theorized that conceited peoples cling to their clichés longest, just as conceited individuals do. And who are the conceited peoples? One cannot flinch from offering a provisional list, subject to anybody's dissent. After due thought: Chinese, Great Russians, Parsees, Sikhs, Burmese, Tibetans, French, Swiss, Italians (notably the Venetians), Hungarians, South African Boers. The Mexicans are on their way to the list but not there yet. The Japanese are too realistic for any such foolishness. Some black African peoples might be added in a decade or so. Some class groups in Prussia, India, Spain, Peru, perhaps England, might be added, but they do not determine total ethnic clichés.

Nor is the cliché necessarily wicked. As has been shown, it is primarily a direct form of communication among groups of people, a signal rather than a thought. The cliché-users may be innocent, conceited, playful, careerist, compulsive, traditional, traitorous, or whatever, but in accepting the cliché they have unwittingly closed a whole area of speculative thought which they instinctively and often violently refuse to reopen. It is to be hoped that these areas have been reopened an inch or two in the foregoing. For some clichés lead to the pit. With slaves.

Other clichés are harmless, true, but a free people must learn to distinguish. The clichés of the children, primarily founded on the bleary, unfocused unreality of TV-watching and music, and being ignored by their parents, are probably harmless. The clichés of the Negro jokers, when the whole Negro community resolves to ignore them, will be harmless. The clichés of the professors are sure to be obsolete a year later when the associate professor destroys the professor. The Fascist clichés of George Wallace are not harmless. And why do decent men such as the Kennedys have to be assassinated? Assassination usually, or perhaps always, derives from the cliché in the mind of the assassin, against normality. How delightful if this arrangement could be reversed.

The practical joke on society is now so common that it is a cliché. I first heard of this satire from a man who said, thirty-five years ago, during the Depression: "Why should I worry? All I have to do is fall down on the street and I'll be taken care of." He was a very self-possessed man. His singular mischievous insight has since become a great cultural design, with the noblest of motives. Society feels committed to care for anybody who simply falls down, honestly or dishonestly, and says, "What are you going to do about it?"

This policy may be desirable as long as the society can afford it. But it leads to the inevitable human inversion. The clever become pastmasters in every bureaucratic nuance of the cry "Help!" and of falling down, while the unclever or honest cannot get out the word until they literally fall down, if then. When weakness is a strength, and strength a weakness, the world is upside down.

A special inversion has infected the Negro community. Here the black Supreme Court Justice, the black Senator from Massachusetts, the black Mayor of Cleveland are described by the Negro jokers as "Uncle Toms," an opprobrious term for a shameful caricature of a Negro. But of course the caricatures or Uncle Toms are the Black Panthers, perhaps to be called "Tom Panthers" or "Black Toms." For the three eminent Negroes stand tall among men, white or black. The primary objective of some black organizations, for example, the Mau Mau, is to kill such distinguished black men.

This remarkable program was expressed, and heard tolerantly, on radio. On this philosophy, revolutionary students ought to kill the A-students, not the teacher; alcoholics ought to kill teetotalers, not the bartender; average professional athletes ought to kill the stars, not the coach. The idea makes a maniacal sense, a formula for a world in total dissolution. Such ideas are received calmly today, when they should be plainly labeled maniacal.

For those aspiring to be very odd, or atrocious, it must be pointed out that the forms of horror or atrocity are extremely limited, and are ancient clichés, long since discarded by the race. It is the natural and instinctive that is infinitely various and relatively resistant to the cliché. Every madman expresses a solitary uniqueness; therefore, it is strange that all madmen sound very much the same. The most remarkable discoveries about phenomena and events will be made by those who open up to them most simply and "normally." Revering an old lady can be inspiring and enlightening; raping her would be, after the shock of abnormality, boring. To admire a young girl's eyes is a subtly up-lifting pleasure; to remove them and eat them would be, after the shock, disgusting. The current experiments in perversion make one think of eating toilet paper and using pancakes on the toilet. Novel as these two sound, as soon as they are articulated they become cliches, fossils, the dead residue of ideas that were not ideas to start with. Such ideas are born dead.

The function of the cliché, ultimately, is to eviscerate what was once miraculously alive, mysterious, and bewitching. True understanding does not turn reality into clichés. Partial understanding, as between husbands and wives, often makes them both clichés, and unbearable to one another. At some point they then consciously adopt the mask of the reiterated cliché. They become closed subjects, hence clichés, but not really.

Superficially, as in a classroom, even this planet can be described as closed, with its shallow atmosphere of oxygen, its partial covering of oxygen mixed with hydrogen as water, and its compulsive gravity. Truly hypersensitive youths may some day revolt against these non-negotiable limitations of oxygen, water, and gravity, and also the monotony of the daily revolution of the planet, and its circling around the Sun, locked in a tyranny that should invite the youths to the symbolic destruction of the nearest planetarium, in default of being able to get their hands on the Establishment, the Sun.

The really fastidious youth, spurning this planet and solar system, would not be comforted by escape to the Moon or Venus, but only to some other solar system where oxygen is considered hopelessly vulgar.

The Earth, however, is subject to continuous radiation, permitting photosynthesis and also occasional mutations and evolution. It is in fact open to the universe of which it is a very small part. Its revolutions producing night and day, and its tipping on its axis producing the four seasons have never struck me as a bore. Along with the whole solar system it is spinning around with the whole galaxy. And the whole galaxy is whirling through space on some unknown errand.

This chilling picture does not awe the cliché-makers tightly hugging themselves in their ratholes somewhere in this magnificent planet but it makes them, not the planet, the cliché.

In the end, the whole is master. We have joined in these pages in some closed revolutions of the parts, frantic circlings in tiny orbits spouting tiny flames. The whole is still mysterious and indescribable, and perhaps it was a waste of time to describe the cliché parts. In that case, forgive me.

But aha! The whole, that is, the universe, reminds me that it is not making jokes or forgiving anybody, ever. I withdraw the apology. Should the whole have already decided to destroy all the little closed clichés, and finally pick its moment of absolute fatigue, don't come to me. I'll be hiding, hoping that the universe doesn't mistake me for one of the cliché-masters. "I'm not human," I will cry, if cornered, "I believe in you."

Metaphors and Similes

Metaphors and Similes

Jargon

Jargon

Life Styles

Life Styles

Idea Clichés

Idea Clichés

Idea Clichés

Idea Clichés